ALONE IN WONDERLAND

CHRISTINE REED

If you see yourself here,
this book is for you.

With love.

Prologue

MY PARENTS WANTED TO RAISE A STRONG, INDEPENDENT WOMAN. I guess some might say they succeeded, though they may have thought I took the whole independence thing too far. I'm twenty-eight years old. I've been single for most of the last decade. I live in a 2003 Dodge Ram passenger van whose seats and carpet have been gutted and replaced with an unfinished plywood floor and a slightly-longer-and-only-slightly-wider-than-twin-size bunk. My home isn't big enough to share—neither is my bed.

I live this way by choice, not out of desperation. Try explaining that one to my father. My parents had such high hopes for me. I had a lot of potential. I tested well enough on kindergarten IQ tests to be skipped to the first grade at age five. I excelled through high school and took advanced placement classes. I could have been a doctor or a lawyer. Now I'm voluntarily unemployed.

My life isn't glamorous by any means, but I have what I need and go where I want. Taking care of myself is second nature by now. I bought the passenger van off an older couple in Las Vegas for $3,500, and it was love at first sight. She's black, mysterious, and hideously nondescript—the kind of van I was told to stay far away from as a kid. I named her Celeste as an homage to the night sky and celestial bodies we would soon be sleeping under. She's loud and clunky and she hates when I drive in the mountains. We've gotten stranded together a few times—her fault—but I can't stay mad at her.

Celeste and I arrived in Seattle just a few days ago, three months after quitting my job. I've been feeling out of place every moment since then. Seattle is a shiny city filled with goal-oriented young professionals and busy businesspeople. My hairy armpits and baby-wipe baths aren't relevant here. I've spent the last few nights with a friend of a friend, who reminisces about the nomadic life she left behind to become a city dweller. The sky-high rent makes it impossible for her to wander long or often.

I'm planning to get out of the city and go hiking on the Wonderland Trail in the next couple days, but there are a few things to sort out before I go. In between researching the permitting system, deciding how many calories to pack, and inspecting the old backpacking gear in my trunk, I keep an eye on the dating market in the greater Seattle area—by swiping. I'm not looking for a partner in crime, just a few hours of entertainment.

I match with Dean while sitting on a bench across from Snoqualmie Falls. The people-watcher in me (and the waterfall enthusiast) enjoys destinations like this one. Parking lots and sidewalk ramps make the falls an accessible attraction for all kinds of visitors. There's a short hiking trail, but most of the visitors are happy to take a picture from the railing and head back to their cars. I stay all day listening to the cascading song of the 268-foot falls. It's a soundtrack of tranquility to accompany my virtual check-ins with friends around the country and shopping for a suitable date.

Dean is a doctor. He's British, forty-six, salt and pepper hair. He's written and published a book about polyamory, and he is way out of my league. My profile is filled with photos in front of Half Dome in Yosemite Valley and on top of fourteeners in Colorado. It showcases my long tangle of dark hair and genuine smile. My profile reads:

> Veggie-Oriented/Environmentalist/Positive Energy Source/Lover/Hiker/Yogi/Runner/Slack-liner/Climber/High on Life/No Drugs Necessary

> Hoping to fall in love with a real dirtbag. Let's do something worth staying another day for.
> #vanlife

What kind of doctor self-identifies as a dirt-bag? And does he know what #vanlife is? If I were trying to attract a successful medical professional, this profile (and this life) isn't how I would go about it. We exchange a few messages; through which I decide he doesn't seem to be a murderer. He invites me to a casual wine bar in the city and I agree to meet him there. I neglect to mention that I don't drink—it probably doesn't matter.

Back in the van, I inventory my wardrobe. I'm not sure I own an appropriate outfit for a midday wine bar date with a doctor in Seattle. In 100-degree weather. The only semi-dressy clothing I own is black. A silky, flowing, cold-shoulder top with long loose sleeves and dark-wash skinny jeans are going to have to suffice. It's not exactly a summer outfit. I throw it on anyway and head toward the city.

I'm sweating profusely and holding my hair away from

my neck as I drive. I don't want to tie it in a rubber band, lest I arrive for our date with an unsightly ponytail bump. Celeste has a new water pump and thermostat, but she still gets a little testy when the temps are in the nineties. As we get into the city, sweltering heat radiates from the asphalt and the engine temperature gauge suddenly shoots into the red zone. I pull into the parking lot of a drugstore, a couple miles from the wine bar.

I don't have time to deal with this right now!

Looking at the clock, I send Dean a quick text.

Might be 5 minutes late.

It's time to walk. With my cute pointy-toe black flats and a swipe of melty coral lipstick, I walk through two miles of Seattle grunge. I pass homeless encampments and dirty alleyways with my head held high and sweat dripping between my shoulder blades. The dank garbage stink of summer in the city fills my nostrils. The top of my right shoe rubs an angry red patch just above my toes. With every step, the pain intensifies.

At no point during the march do I consider that this man isn't worth my time or suffering. As independent as I want to be, my mind still traipses down the road of possibility. I imagine a future as the wife of a hot older polyamorous Seattleite doctor with a British accent. A girl can dream.

At the wine bar, we smile with recognition and order drinks before finding a couple empty chairs on the patio. Nowhere in Seattle has air conditioning, so it's all but unbearable to sit indoors. At least on the street-facing patio the movement of cars driving by creates an illusion of air circulation. Dean's face is damp with sweat as he greets me. We're on equal footing.

"Wow, you look really beautiful." His eyes crinkle at the

corners when he smiles but he struggles to focus them on me.

"Thanks." I study his face. He looks older, more tired than in his photos.

"Like, really really beautiful." Dean's words slur together as he puts a hand on my thigh.

Is he drunk?!

I glance around the patio. A man sitting across the way is trying not to notice us. I am acutely aware of the obvious age difference between us and of Dean's hand on my leg. Others around us continue with their conversations and glasses of sauv blanc, oblivious to Dean's lascivious behavior.

A server sets down one glass of wine and one of water on the table between us. I down the icy water like a shot, feeling the chill all the way to my stomach. Dean tastes the red wine. How many of those has he had today?

"What do you think about going back to my place for a coffee?" he proposes, after only a few minutes of awkward conversation.

"Hmm…" I make a non-committal sound.

Absolutely, under no circumstances whatsoever am I going back to this guy's house. But how do I escape this situation unscathed? I can't just say no, can I? Should I just leave now? Should I call him out for being drunk? I don't know if he's an angry drunk, so I want to play it safe and try not to set him off.

I've been wasted on a first date before. My hypocrisy is glaring. But irony doesn't negate the danger of the situation. I'm going to have to walk back to the van—without being followed.

"I'm going to use the bathroom and then we can go back to my place." Dean is persistent, bordering on belligerent.

"Okay." I nod absently.

As soon as he's gone from the table, I crane my neck to watch him walk into the restroom. In my rush to vacate the premises I nearly overturn my chair. Out the front door, over one block and around the corner, I keep watch over my shoulder as I go. My heart pounds mercilessly in my chest, my breathing is heavy, sweaty tendrils of hair wrap around my neck. Once I'm two blocks away from the bar I pull out my phone and dial a friend. Holding the hot screen against my cheek, I explain my situation and she agrees to stay on the line with me until I reach Celeste.

"The guy was totally tanked," I pant into the phone.

"I'm glad you got out of there safely." My friend is sympathetic.

"Yeah, turns out, I'm not destined to be the wife of a hot older polyamorous Seattleite doctor with a British accent. Unless there's another one of those around here somewhere." We crack up as I tromp down the street.

———

If one bad date were enough to stop me from swiping, I would have given up the app game years ago. Over the following days, I hope the men of Seattle can redeem themselves. No more doctors, published authors, or British men in their forties. I stay in my lane.

A few days later, lying in bed in the back of the van, I sift through the monotony of bad mirror selfies and status pics with expensive cars. It's early evening, but the stifling heat hangs stubbornly around me. My tank top is damp, and the musky smell of my body fills the small cabin space. I swipe right on Tate, 30. He has shoulder length brown hair and a daring grin. His photos exude immeasurable charm. He's a certified paragliding guide. He messages promptly.

T: *Nice to match up! You are also #vanlife?*

C: *Yes! Are you currently? Or getting ready?*

T: *Yeah. It's a shithole though. It was livable, but basic. So, I planned home improvement.*

T: *That's code for, take stuff out, and sleep amongst tools on a thermarest bc summer is hella busy flying.*

C: *Hahaha. I definitely moved into my van before it was functional and that was a fun twist on adventure.*

T: *How long are you in the area?*

C: *Indefinitely. I have no plan. Where are you bus building?*

T: *Kinda squatting on my boss's property—interesting situation.*

C: *Well that sounds very glamorous. I'm just pondering finding a spot in the city to squat for the night.*

T: *Come to the burbs?*

C: *You got a parking spot available for the semi-homeless?*

T: *Yeah, what rig are you driving?*

C: *Just a van—old Dodge Ram.*

T: *Go to poo poo point trailhead.*

C: *Is that a joke…?*

A cursory online search for Poo Poo Point Trailhead turns up a renowned paragliding launch point in the small town of Issaquah. I check my messages again.

T: *How about this. We hike poo poo point by night. Sleep there. Fly tandem early morning. Orrrrrrrrrr We drive up. Van crash. Fly tomorrow.*

C: *Yes.*

T: *I am grubby. Do I need to shower?*

C: *It's been 95 and I haven't showered so you shouldn't unless I can too.*

I bolt from my bunk and through the van to the driver's seat. Paragliding isn't on my short list of things to do, but it's hard to imagine passing up the offer. I type Poo Poo Point into my phone.

It's almost midnight when I arrive in Issaquah. Tate greets me with a bear hug and throws a mess of paragliding gear in the back of the van next to the bed. He's just as handsome as his photos and his smile is just as wide. His thick Minnesotan accent comes as a surprise—do they say *hella* in Minnesota? He directs me up a narrow winding dirt road and we park at the top of Tiger Mountain. The stars twinkle overhead, affirming my spontaneous escape from the city.

We climb over the mountain of gear to the tiny bed. It's a tight fit, but we lie comfortably next to each other. I've spent the better part of the last three months alone and his warm body is a pleasant change. By my standards he's hardly grungy at all. I wonder if he thinks I am. There isn't much time for talking before lights out.

Tate's alarm sounds in the pre-dawn stillness and he leaps to action. Before I realize what's happening, he has clambered out the side doors and started pacing around outside the van. I squint my bleary eyes at my watch—it's five o'clock. After months of blissful unemployment, I've forgotten how it feels to be violently alerted to the beginning of the day.

He opens the door and crawls back into bed. "The wind isn't right," he explains.

"Oh, okay. So, we wait?" I hope this doesn't mean the flight is off.

"Yeah, we wait. It'll change," Tate says with absolute authority.

Twenty minutes later he's outside checking the wind again. And twenty minutes after that. The sun colors the sky and birds chirp in the trees around us. Around seven, the wind shifts. Tate sets to work. He drags a parachute, harnesses, and helmets over to the large bald peak of Tiger Mountain. From the launch point, I look out over the quaint town of Issaquah and the endless farmland beyond.I wring my hands and offer to help though I don't have a clue what needs to be done. My stomach somersaults. A hint of fear sneaks into the back of my mind. He hands me a harness and a helmet. I put them on. One step closer to jumping off a mountain.

What am I thinking? I don't even know this guy. He could be anybody.

Tate leans over and tugs on the straps of my harness. My stomach flutters at his touch. He nods approvingly. He launches into the spiel of a seasoned guide. He explains how we're going to strap our harnesses together, with our bodies in much the same position we spent the night—spooning. Then we will run, run, run as fast as we can toward the edge of the cliff and the parachute will catch air behind us. If all goes well, as we reach the precipice we will run into air and glide away. Just like that.

"And if it doesn't go well?" I squeak.

"I'll say STOP RUNNING, and we'll try again," Tate says.

No big deal. I try my best to swallow the lump in my throat.

In one fluid movement he pulls me in close, turns me around, and clips onto the back of my harness.

We're facing the cliff and Tate whispers in my ear. "Are

you ready?"

Those words at this proximity are electric and sexy.

"Ready as I'll ever be." I nod.

"RUN RUN RUN RUN!" Tate shouts gleefully from right behind me. I can hear the big goofy grin on his face.

I pedal as hard and fast as I can. He matches my step. The weight of the parachute resists our efforts, but we slowly gain ground.

"RUN RUN RUN! Keep running!" His voice is loud and urgent.

It doesn't feel like we're about to fly. He doesn't sound confident. It's my fault. I can't run fast enough. I push into my legs, but my quadriceps are already on fire. My breath is ragged, and I drive my arms forward and back. We've only moved twenty feet or so.

"STOP!" he yells.

We stop. I look back to see the parachute behind us, quickly losing air. It falls to the ground. I shrink in shame. We failed. I failed. Tate quickly unhooks from me and starts dragging the parachute back to our original position. He has the exuberant presence of a child—this is what he loves.

"Alright, let's go," he calls to me.

I realize I've been standing stock-still at the end of the runway watching him prepare to fly again. I hurry back into position, turning myself around this time so he can place the carabiners.

We run again. This time the parachute fills with air and pulls away from the ground. By the time we reach the end of the runway, white pillowy sails block out the sky above. My feet lift from the grassy mountain top, leaving me pedaling in midair on an invisible bicycle.

We are flying.

Tate lets out a triumphant whoop and my stomach finally unclenches. He steers the parachute this way and that while instructing me to sit back into my harness.

My body shouldn't be able to do this, but it feels so natural. There was no gut-wrenching drop, no pull of gravity—only the magical lift of the parachute. I'm in ecstasy. A dreamy smile plays on my face as Tate swooshes the craft from left to right and back again.

"Do you want to feel the Gs?" he asks.

"Okay!" I yell back.

I'm not sure what he means, but I've come this far.

He pulls up and down on the handles and we swing in the harness, forward and back, the parachute shifting angles above us. I experience a moment of weightlessness that takes my breath away. When we land firmly back in our harnesses, laughter bubbles up.

"Do you want to steer?" he offers.

"Yes!" I can't believe I'm allowed.

"This is left, and this is right." He takes my hands and places them on the handles.

I pull timidly on one and then the other, testing the resistance. With more confidence I swing us widely to the left before pivoting back to the right in a large gentle arc.

"Wow! You're a natural." Tate's voice is assuring. He's the expert.

"Ya think?" I beam with pride.

"Yeah, you wanna travel the world and fly with me?" He laughs.

"Maybe!"

I do. I really do. It's hard to imagine anything more magical than this.

"We've got to get ready to land!" Tate reaches for the

controls and I drop my hands to my sides.

The earth grows nearer as Tate steers us toward a grassy patch behind the trailhead. The landing zone is groomed for paragliders and offers a large, soft target. My head is swimming with the possibility of it all. Traveling the world with a handsome stranger. Learning how to fly and doing it every day. What kind of fantasy life is that?

Tate brings us to the ground expertly and we run out the momentum in only a few steps. Once we're disconnected, I turn to see his wide grin and he pulls me in for a kiss. Our breath intermingles as our lips connect. His muscles ripple under his shirt and his unwashed scent is intoxicating. The energy between us is heavy with promise.

Day 0: August 1, 2018

Issaquah, WA → Mt. Rainier National Park

I PEER THROUGH THE PRE-DAWN LIGHT AT THE FACE RESTING NEXT TO mine. The bed isn't wide enough for me to pull away and get a good look, so I gaze instead at Tate's cheekbone. As if through a microscope, I study his peach fuzz. His warm breath soothes me. We hadn't seen each other in the five days since our flight but I couldn't bear to spend another night alone, and he obliged my request. In sleep he is quite beautiful.

Tate's offer to run away together still hangs in the air but it's already lost its shine. I don't know if I could tolerate his Minnesotan accent for months on end, in places where we might be the only English-speakers for miles. I've been telling myself for so long that I'm better off alone, working endlessly to squash the desire for romantic attachment, so it doesn't feel right to abandon my solo journey and tag along with someone else's.

I suspect he feels the same way. Disconnected. To him I would be a temporary solution. Not the woman he is searching for, but a woman. Any woman will do.

His eyes snap open at the loud chimes of my alarm. It's 4:01 a.m. and the notification reads "Go get permits!!!" I think of the long day ahead, made longer by the time spent tangled in the sheets last night.

I'm heading to the Paradise Climbing Information Center in Mt. Rainier National Park to try for a walk-up permit to hike the Wonderland Trail. If I'm lucky enough to get a permit I'll be gone for a couple weeks, but there's no guarantee. Maybe I won't be able to get a permit at all, maybe I won't come back to Seattle.

"See you in two weeks," I offer, whether it's the truth or not.

As Tate steps out of the van into the early dawn we exchange tired, knowing smiles. He knew what he was getting into hanging around with a woman like me. You can hardly expect stability and partnership from someone who agrees to jump off a cliff on a first date. He never looks back as he walks away. I brush off the creeping feeling of loss—I knew what I was getting into too.

Lying on my bed, I wiggle into my new gray hiking pants. They're the same as my black ones from last season but one size bigger. I recently broke down and finally bought the next size, a surrender to the weight I've put on in the last few months on the road.

I stand in a hunched position and move to the front of the van. Plopping into the driver's seat, I take in the silence around me. Tate has already disappeared around the corner and it feels as if he was never here. Celeste rumbles to life in the pre-dawn and we're off together into the unknown. It's just the two of us again, we're comfortable that way. I pull up the directions to Paradise Climbing Information Center on my phone and set it in the cup holder for the three-hour drive.

Paradise isn't the closest location to request a permit, but it opens thirty minutes earlier than the others. I cross my fingers that those thirty minutes will be enough of a head-start to plan my trip before the next person can get in to apply. The Wonderland Trail is a ninety-three-mile circumnavigation of Mt. Rainier, a stunning snow-capped 14,000-foot mountain in Washington state, and permits are in high demand. A select few are awarded by lottery each spring and even fewer are reserved for walk-up applicants with enough free time on their hands to show up in the wee hours of the morning ready to go.

During the first hour of the drive I'm buzzing with excitement. This will be my first multi-night backpacking trip since my attempted thru-hike of the Appalachian Trail three years ago. A lot has changed in that time. I look at myself in the rear-view mirror and the woman who stepped foot on the Appalachian Trail in March 2015 looks back at me.

My circumstances have changed but the reason for this trip feels oddly familiar. In the last three years I have become more and more isolated. I have walked away from familial obligations, friendships that did not serve me (and maybe some that did), and romantic entanglements that ventured too close to serious territory.

Back then I was trying so desperately to prove that I wasn't who I was being told to be. I had boldly set out to do the most outrageous thing I could think of. When I left for the Appalachian Trail, I wanted to become someone who was about something. I wanted to be a woman who found joy in independence. It didn't take long for the joy to wear off and the independence to become a burden. I hope backpacking is the joy I've been missing, because that would be easy to get back.

———

I arrive in the Paradise Visitor Center parking lot a few minutes after seven in the morning. There are only two other vehicles and I hope some other hiker hasn't beaten me to the punch. A group of eight hikers appear to be preparing for a multi-day trip, stuffing things into packs and comparing gear. Any group larger than two that manages to successfully organize an activity together is impressive to me.

In the Information Center I find two female rangers staffing the desk and not a tourist or aspiring backpacker in sight. Feeling as though my odds have somehow increased, I realize that I have no Plan B. If I'm unable to get a permit, I suppose I'll call it a day and head home. Wherever that is. As I approach the counter, one of the rangers greets me over a computer.

"What can I do for you?" She stands at the ready with mouse in hand.

"I'd like to hike the Wonderland Trail." I get right to the point.

"How long do you want to hike?" she asks.

"As long as possible," I answer, misunderstanding the question.

"Like, how far are you trying to go?" Her eyes narrow.

"Oh! I want to hike the whole thing. In as many days as possible," I clarify. The idea that someone would acquire a permit to hike only a portion of the trail seems obvious now but hadn't previously occurred to me.

"Just you?" she questions.

"Yup." I try to keep the pride out of my voice.

On the cultural spectrum of independence there is a line which says, "women stop here." It can be found somewhere between "well-educated and capable of supporting oneself financially" and "well-equipped and capable in the wilderness." Flirting with and stepping over that line has become my act of defiance. Defiance to my parents, of course, and to society. I bristle at the unfairness of my female body and the social conditioning that tells me and everyone around me that some things just aren't safe for me because of it.

"Okay." She pulls out a Wilderness Trip Planner map and flattens it on the desk between us.

The various backcountry campsites are indicated by triangle symbols and a dashed line represents the Wonderland Trail encircling the peak and glaciers of Mt. Rainier. The map is cartoonish and simplistic—it hardly seems representative of the grand adventure I'm about to embark upon.

I know the likelihood of scoring a permit goes up with increased flexibility so when she asks where I want to start I tell her it doesn't matter, and when she asks if I want my hike to begin today or tomorrow I say either one.

"How many miles a day do you want to hike?" She looks me up and down and raises an eyebrow. I know I don't look as experienced as I am. I wonder if the rangers make bets on hikers' success.

"Probably around ten?" I answer in the form of a question.

Hiking ten miles a day will have me finishing the trail in nine days. I'd like to stay longer, but I don't want to seem like an amateur who can't hike ten miles. The ranger might think they'll find me dead out there. I fall somewhere between the athletic hikers I'm always comparing myself to and the absolute disaster I've worked so hard to leave behind. I worry I will perpetually live in this in-between space and always present as such.

"Well. Let me see what's available today and tomorrow, and we can start from there." She studies the screen in front of her.

Not surprisingly, nothing within a one-day hike of the trailhead at Longmire Visitor Center on the southwest side of the park is available. Longmire is easily the most popular starting point for Wonderland thru-hikers. She moves on to the Sunrise area and I light up at the memory of day-hiking the Fremont Lookout Trail from there last week. That hike was the original inspiration for my decision to hike the Wonderland Trail.

It's a fleeting thought, as she informs me that the Sunrise area is completely booked as well. The ranger sighs again and continues looking back and forth from the map to the computer. She moves the tip of a pen to the Mowich Lake Campground on the west side of the map and moves clockwise around the circle, referring back to the computer screen with each point of the pen. She starts to shake her head, clearly convinced we're running out of options.

"What if I hike the opposite direction?" I ask.

She begins searching counterclockwise from Mowich Lake, and it appears we may have a winner.

Next thing I know, my stomach flutters as she begins circling camps. As she finds available sites, she asks a landslide of questions. Can I hike twelve miles in one day? Would I be okay with staying at the same camp two nights in a row before moving on? Yes, and yes! I'll do whatever I need to do.

"Can I stay at Indian Bar? And Summerland too?" I make this request on the advice of a friend. The ranger circles both. I would find out later that these are the two most highly sought out campsites on the trail, and few hikers get to stay at both.

When I leave the information center there are eleven campsites with my name on them. My hike doesn't begin until tomorrow, so I have the rest of the day to prepare.

———

In the parking lot, I divide my food supply into three caches to be dropped off around the park. Mt. Rainier has three main visitor areas, all of which are accessible via the Wonderland Trail. Hikers have the option to mail or drop off food caches to each location and then pick them up during their thru-hike, significantly decreasing their starting pack weight. Before leaving Seattle, I purchased two clear plastic totes specifically for this purpose.

I fill a stuff sack with the first four days of food and test the weight. My daily ramen, oatmeal and granola bars aren't terribly heavy, thank goodness. Memories of my hefty food bag on the Appalachian Trail haunt my backpacking dreams. There is a saying in the backpacking community—"you pack your fears." I'm not afraid of hunger like I used to be.

Twelve miles away on a winding mountain road is the Wilderness Information Center in Longmire. Carrying my plastic tote of rations with its bright pink lid, I enter the building and am greeted by a friendly, bright-eyed ranger. I make note that all three rangers I have encountered so far have been women.

"I just got my Wonderland permit, and I need to drop off a food cache," I tell her.

"Sure! Did they tell you about trail conditions?" She smiles warmly.

"No... why?" I ask. Last I checked, it's a beautiful sunny day in August.

She opens a map with a flourish and says, "there are

several river crossings which have been a bit treacherous, because of the heavy glacial melt. We've had unusually hot temperatures for a couple of weeks now, and some of the bridges have been washing out."

Uh, say what?

I know how to ford a river in theory but have always thought the idea of submerging my shoes and socks halfway through a day of backpacking sounds like the kind of fresh hell someone might create specifically with me in mind.

"We had a death in the park a few days ago. Near Mystic Lake camp, crossing the White River," she continues, pointing casually to the deadly river on the map. "So be careful in that area. But, if water is coming over *any* bridge, DO NOT cross it."

"What should I do?" I demand.

I'm out in the middle of the wilderness and I come to an unsafe bridge, and what? I live here now?

"Wait for the water level to go down before crossing," she says coolly.

"Oh. Is the water level changing that much?" I ask.

"It's usually lowest in the morning, so if you can't find a safer place to cross, stay there until it goes back down," she says.

"Like camp by the river?" I clarify.

Unacceptable! I just spent thirty-five minutes obtaining a piece of paper telling me exactly where I am permitted to sleep for the next twelve days. She can't possibly be suggesting I set up camp randomly on the banks of a river.

"Yes, if that's what you have to do. Don't risk your life to make your reservations. That's part of the problem, people trying to follow their permit, instead of thinking about safety," she says.

How many hikers start the trail thinking the permit is the law, no exceptions? It seems like a crucial distinction to make, letting people know there are potentially dangerous situations that might supersede rule-following. National Parks strike a strange balance between preservation of the natural world (which is inherently dangerous) and accessibility for the masses (who are inherently underqualified). Many of us tend to lean on the "rules" which were obviously devised to keep us safe and forget that these places are still wild.

"Anything else I should know?" My stomach tightens as I brace for an explanation of gaping ravines, exposed cliff walks, killer marmots! Even with my backpacking experience, I might be out of my league here. Maybe the Pacific Northwest is more hardcore than I thought.

"Nope, that's about it." She nods, obviously oblivious to the shock factor of the information she has relayed.

"What about wildlife in the park? What's the deal with bears around here?" I ask.

"We only have black bears in the area and have never had a violent bear incident in the history of the park," she says. I breathe a sigh of relief. "And all of the designated camping areas have bear poles to hang your food. There is a mama bear and some cubs who have been hanging around in Summerland. Are you staying there?" She glances at my permit, where Summerland is listed clear as day. "When you get into camp, you'll want to make sure to hang your food bag right away, because they've been caught a few times rummaging in unattended backpacks."

"Got it! Seems easy enough." Now I'm confident. I've spent a decent amount of time in black bear country and know that with the most basic of precautions, they pose little to no threat. "So, then I give you my food cache and I'm good to go?"

"Yup, we'll make sure it's labeled and put it in the book and then you'll pick it up here when you come back through," she confirms.

I hand over my plastic container and thank the ranger for the information. Standing at the counter and looking over the map, I eavesdrop as she talks with an older woman who had been waiting somewhat impatiently to ask about day hikes that aren't too hard on the knees.

———

Back in the van, I refer to my *National Geographic Adventure Edition Atlas* and its tiny, zoomed-in version of Mt. Rainier National Park. On the exact opposite side of the park is White River Campground—about fifty miles away. According to my borrowed copy of *Hiking the Wonderland Trail* by Tami Asars, I must only take my supply package as far as the gate and it will magically transport to the campground cache container before I arrive on foot.

At the gate of the White River area of the park my cell phone starts going off. It's the first time I've had reception all morning and a barrage of *Are you there?* and *Did you get a permit?* and *When will you be back?* texts flood in. I show the gate attendant my national park pass and ask where I can drop off my food cache. He indicates a small hut beyond the entrance, and I continue through.

A row of diagonal spaces line the right-hand side of the road. There I rummage around the back of the van, grabbing the last plastic tote from where it slid beneath the bed. I nearly jump out of my skin when I turn around with my bucket of food and find myself in uncomfortable proximity with a construction worker who's come over to say hello. He's probably around my dad's age, although he looks a lot older—working construction is considerably harder on the body than anything my dad ever did for a living.

As a young woman in the world I have been told time and time again men are dangerous; a woman alone is a target, keep your guard up, don't talk to strangers. The hairs on my neck prickle to attention and I force my clenched jaw into something like a smile. My stomach rolls over and I search for an exit route. My disdain for the fear I have been taught to operate under can't seem to override these visceral reactions.

"Are those solar panels on your van?" He flashes me a conspiratorial grin.

"Y-yeah," I stutter. Relief instantly washes over me, leaving only annoyance behind. Talking about van building and logistics is not on my agenda today. Slamming the door behind me, I disengage and head toward the ranger station. I drop off my second food cache and am assured it will be waiting for me at the White River Campground when I arrive eight days later.

I try my best to be invisible when walking back to the van, but alas, it's always difficult to be invisible when it suits me. The construction guy is still standing beside my home, eagerly awaiting my return.

"Hey, I just wanted to say, if you're traveling around in your van, there's some good places to stay for free, I can tell you. I used to stay in my van before I started working here." His face is open and earnest, as if there is nothing more appealing to a young woman traveling solo than the idea of a strange older man directing her to some great secluded spots where she can sleep.

I must constantly remind myself that most men don't have any idea about the type of weird, sick stuff that flashes through a woman's mind when assessing the potential danger of a situation. He's probably a nice guy, trying to give a gal pro-tips on the stealthy van life. Pro-tips she didn't ask for.

"Oh, I'm actually headed out on the Wonderland Trail, so I'll be parking at the trailhead. Thanks though!" I cringe internally. I probably shouldn't tell this dude where I'll be, but chances are he isn't coming out on a trail to hunt me down. Plus, if I can put a quick end to the interaction and get the heck out of here, he may forget I exist.

"Yeah, back in the day, my friend used to have a bumper sticker that said, 'If you're not vanning, you're not living.' Isn't that great?" He chuckles at the joke.

I refrain from rolling my eyes and resign myself to the conversation.

"Yep."

He insists on talking me through some great camp spots and circling them on my map before bidding me farewell and heading back to work.

———

The road from the White River entrance to Mowich Lake is about seventy-five miles and follows a painfully indirect route. It passes through the self-proclaimed "charming" town of Carbonado. A sign at the fork in the road indicates Mowich Lake Road, and my heart skips a beat: the adventure begins! Chugging up ten miles of dirt road, I see only one other car and start to think I'm going to have a beautifully secluded evening of camping and lake time. To my surprise, the dirt road opens to a sizable parking lot that is at least half full on a Wednesday afternoon. The car camping area is complete with two pit toilets and ten first-come first-serve gravel pad campsites.

I claim a spot with my little backpacking tent in the area

designated for Wilderness Permit holders. Eager to meet other Wonderland hikers, I soon discern that tonight may not be the night. Only one campsite nearby appears to be that of a true backpacker, but they're nowhere to be found. The other gravel squares are occupied by standing-room tents, plastic totes of kitchen gear, and groups of children running to and fro. Obviously, these are car campers.

I mosey over to the lake to find a quieter spot to relax in the late afternoon sun. Mowich Lake is situated on the north side of the campsite with a wall of trees blocking the view from one to the other. I take the trail through the greenery and am overcome when I see it for the first time, with its gentle tree-covered hillside rising from the far edge of the water and reflecting in the crystal blue surface.

The trail continues to the right, past several groups of swimmers and sunbathers enjoying the closest access points of the lake. They are laughing—splashing and floating in the water. I sit at the edge of the lake, feeling particularly alone and wondering what it would be like to be here with someone. Stepping off on the trail first thing in the morning with someone. Floating in the lake with someone.

Before returning to my campsite I stop at the Mowich Lake Ranger Station and snoop around a bit. It's more of a cabin than a ranger station, with a privy around back and a food cache on the porch. A trail log in a tattered plastic bag is nailed to the worn wooden doorframe. It only takes a few minutes to read through what amounts to daily weather reports and a few bear sightings from previous hikers. The lack of narrative and imagination in the log is a bit disappointing.

Trail logs are a vital cultural part of the Appalachian Trail; hikers divulge their hopes, dreams, and darkest secrets (as well as the recounting of interesting, or not-so-interesting, trail events) to the hiking community. The original purpose of the logs was to create a record of those passing through in case a concerned loved one or the authorities were compelled to track down a hiker in the wilderness. The evolution into a forum for all other creative pursuits is simply a function of the long trail doldrums, which must not have time enough to come to a head in ninety-three miles.

I scrawl my entry in the log in true AT fashion, disregarding the pattern laid out by previous Wonderland hikers. Maybe future hikers will be inspired to leave more behind.

Dear Diary,

4 months ago, I quit my job and set out to find something greater. Last week, I came to Mt. Rainier National Park for the first time and fell in love.

This morning I woke up @ 4 am in Issaquah, drove to Paradise to get my permits, dropped off food caches in Longmire & White River and after many arduous hours have arrived in this utopia for the evening.

I am so jazzed to be on the Wonderland Trail. Hoping to spend 12 days in wonder and hopefully make a friend or 2.

> Best Day Ever!
> -Lady Unicorn

Nobody has called me Lady Unicorn in years, but it flows naturally from my left hand. After stuffing the log back into the plastic bag, I hang it on its nail.

The sun slowly sinks toward the trees as I boil and stir a pot of ramen with dehydrated beet and kale chips. Groups of children frolic around me. I crawl into my sleeping bag before 8:30, sure the camp noises will continue around me for another hour at least, but I fall asleep almost instantly. My loneliness is placated by the knowledge that I may sleep when I please, rise when I please, and feed only myself at the end of the day.

Chapter 1

GOING TO COLLEGE WAS NEVER A CHOICE FOR ME—IT WAS A requirement. My parents didn't want me to end up stuck in a hopeless marriage with no skills of my own to fall back on. They wanted to raise a strong independent daughter who could leave her shitty husband if she needed to. It's a funny thought, because my parents were happily married so I don't know why they were so afraid of this unhappy marriage scenario.

My mom never dreamed of leaving my dad, and she could have if she needed to. Even without finishing college. But she always got a wistful look in her eye when she talked about the opportunities she would have had if she had graduated.

Hers wasn't a traditional story of her generation—girl goes to college, girl meets boy, girl drops out of college to get married and have a baby. It was uglier than that. Girl goes to college, girl meets boy, boy empties girl's bank account and leaves town, girl drops out of college because she doesn't have the money to pay her tuition. Then she met my dad.

There are lessons in stories like these. Lessons to be impressed upon daughters. Lessons to be reconciled through the actions of the next generation. So, going to college was never a choice for me. And warnings about boys and their bad intentions weighed on me when I got there.

I was well-suited for higher education; I had loved school since before I was allowed to go. When my brother started kindergarten, I was interminably jealous. Mom had to start playing school at home with me to settle the score. I learned my letters and numbers and was reading and writing long before I turned five. She tried to enroll me a year early for kindergarten, but the school flatly refused to accept me. After another year of school-at-home, I was promptly skipped to first grade within the first two weeks of kindergarten.

My first day of college I was only a few months past seventeen. When I stepped on the campus of University of Arkansas at Little Rock, I was disappointed by its overwhelming lack of timeless Harvard charm. It wasn't like the college TV shows where beautiful coeds drink beer from red plastic cups at Greek-themed parties. There were hardly any beautiful coeds at all. UALR was a commuter school; a place where middle-aged single moms took night classes in hopes of increasing their earning potential.

The stress of going back to college in your forties or fifties looked like crow's feet and frizzy hair and smelled like stale cigarette smoke. I thought being a college student would make me feel older and more mature, but the age and intensity of my classmates had the opposite effect. They all took the thing way too seriously, spending the moments before a test comparing study schedules.

"How many hours did you study for this test?" they would demand with accusatory glares in my direction.

"I spent seventeen hours studying," they would state proudly to all who would hear them.

"I didn't sleep at all last night!" they would compete for the who-is-most-sleep-deprived award.

Graduating from high school and moving on to higher education is held up as a standard of independence in our society but I found it to be a hollow representation. At seventeen I still lived at home, still obeyed my parents' rules, and still sought their approval through good grades. I wanted to live in a dorm, but my school didn't offer much in the way of campus life. Plus, it was made abundantly clear that if anyone were paying for me to live away from home it would be me.

Within the constructs I was raised it was hard to distinguish what true independence looked like. The word had often been used in the context of establishing myself financially—by getting a college education. Those were the prescribed steps, but they left me feeling powerless. My parents decided what school I should go to and where I should live. The school decided what classes I should take and what majors I could choose from. I felt caged, even without the self-awareness to see the box I was in.

————

My shameless flirtations and sexual promiscuity were not just a rebellion against the control of my parents and the college experience; I also needed to free myself from the judgement of my peers. Through the relentless bullying of teenagers, my self-esteem had been brutally dismantled over the four years of high school. I had been told who I was, where I belonged, and how little I was worth. Even after leaving the small town of my youth the voices of my peers told me who I was. My escape could only be found in a man's desire. I needed to know that I was worthy. The key to freedom was rigid and throbbing and in some guy's pants.

Before the heat of summer had worn off my first college semester, a man in the drama department recognized my desperation. I had noticed him between classes, lounging on the sofa reading a book and talking animatedly with other students. He was undeniably handsome with a big toothy grin and an even bigger personality. Even when he was reading a book it was as if he was over-acting what a person reading a book might look like.

The first time we spoke it was like a dream. He plopped down next to me and whispered in my ear. He told me I had caught his eye. How strange...I had been trying to catch his eye for weeks.

A few days later, he asked if I wanted to go somewhere and make out.

"Oh, I don't know... I don't really do things like that..." I was shocked by how forward he was.

"I'm not asking if you want to make love, come make out with me," he pushed. "It's not a big deal."

"Okay," I agreed, not wanting to seem like a prude. A handsome man was interested in me, and I didn't have the luxury of passing up that kind of attention.

He grabbed my hand and led me through the doors to the empty theater, looking back with a wink as he directed me to the front row. We flipped the folding chairs open and sat side by side facing the unoccupied stage. The masculine scent of his cologne was powerful and intoxicating at this proximity. I tried to slow my racing heart. I stared hard at the stage as if something interesting were taking place there, unsure of how to proceed. He leaned in, his hot breath tickling my neck.

"You're very beautiful," he whispered.

My pulse quickened in my chest, my wrists, my ears. I didn't know how to react to such a compliment—I'd never been given one before. The tip of his nose pressed lightly below my ear and my whole body erupted in goosebumps. I closed my eyes as he brought my face toward his and our lips joined. It was the first time a grown man had kissed me. He was confident in his actions and filled with lust, not like the nervous and inexperienced teenage boys I had kissed before.

I was lost in the moment when he pulled away and looked into my eyes. In the shadowy room his features were dark and distinguished.

Why would a man like this be interested in me?

He kissed me again and placed his hand on my thigh. I tensed.

His hand wandered upward, and I pushed it back. He paused.

"Are you a virgin?" he asked, as if this was the only reason I wouldn't want his hand creeping up my leg.

"No, but..." I hesitated.

"How old are you?" A look of understanding dawned on his face.

"Seventeen," I responded, wondering if an older woman would have behaved differently.

"Oh." His look of understanding quickly transformed into one of shock and distrust as if I had revealed a dark secret I had been hiding. He got up and walked out of the room.

For several days, we exchanged uncomfortable glances in the drama corridor. One day he stopped me to whisper that I couldn't tell anyone we had kissed. I was so surprised by his approach that I agreed without thinking and kept walking.

He made a point of ignoring me for weeks after that, until one day when he found me alone on the couch.

"I haven't been able to get you out of my mind," he whispered.

"Huh?" I had been watching him surreptitiously every day and he was doing an excellent job of seeming disinterested.

"Here's my number." He held out a scrap of paper. After I took it, he jumped off the couch as if it were suddenly on fire and marched out of the building. My stomach fluttered as I entered his number into my phone and texted it immediately.

We made plans to meet up the next day and our affair went on for months. We ditched classes to have sex in the deserted theater, always listening for approaching footsteps or a creaking door.

He reminded me constantly that our relationship was a secret. He was ten years my senior and had full custody of his son. He couldn't risk problems with the child's mother, he told me, because she was mentally unstable. His situation was understandably serious, so I only told one friend about our involvement. I loved him, but of course we must keep it covert. I thought he loved me too and imagined after I turned eighteen, we would be together for real. It must have been naïve to think he loved me too.

———

A year later, I had replaced one inappropriate relationship with another. This new man and I had been sleeping together for several months when he insisted that I come to his twenty-seventh birthday. He wanted me to come, even though his girlfriend was going to be there. I was foolishly in love with him, so I agreed to go but when I arrived my stomach was twisted in knots. Social anxiety mixed with the strangeness of the situation like a bad cocktail.

A flirtatious foreign exchange student from Rwanda began pouring whiskey shots, which loosened me up. I tried to convince him my French was abysmal. He wouldn't be deterred, even as I could only understand a few words for every sentence he whispered in my ear. I glanced around to see if my lover noticed this man giving me his best.

My memory cuts out early in the evening. How many shots of whiskey did I drink? How did I end up lying on the bathroom floor with nothing but my tank top on? How long was I lying there paralyzed while my body was touched and penetrated before I dragged my consciousness back from the brink and forced my heavy eyelids open?

I couldn't recall the details; it was like I never possessed them to begin with. I felt certain this information was kept under lock and key in someone else's memory. The glimpses from that night felt so far away from my personal experience—as if I had only seen them in a movie a long time ago. I forgot all but the image of the most terrifying face, suspended over me with the blinding bathroom light shining around like an ironic halo.

I never asked my lover about that night. I didn't want to hear what I already knew. How his real girlfriend had heard me crying out from the next room, or how he had to get down on the bathroom floor and wipe up the blood I had left behind. I wanted to forget how he had banged down the door and threatened to kill the man who assaulted me. I hoped that we could both forget how he had held me, sobbing, in the shower and how in that moment my biggest fear was that he would think less of me. There were large chunks of the evening that I couldn't remember, and the rest I was determined to forget.

Our relationship continued for almost a year after the incident. In the weeks following, we didn't talk about it. He held me while I cried and assured me that he didn't think less of me by continuing to sleep with me. Nothing had changed. I took comfort in his presence, in his affection—while his girlfriend was at work. And I left before she came home.

I was becoming accustomed to the taste of hard liquor when I met a good-looking redneck with a real drinking problem. My best friend was old enough to buy booze and her new guy had an even older best friend, so when the four of us got together, drinking was the activity of choice. When the alcohol was flowing Josephine and James would go find someplace private to have sex, leaving Jack and me to stare at each other.

He may have been ten years older than me, but his style of flirting was childish and sometimes insulting. I wanted to have enough self-respect to turn him down, and for a while I did. But as other more appropriate and more desirable dating prospects continually fell flat, he eventually wore me down. His need to have me made me feel valuable. Maybe not in the way a woman wants to be valued, but it was better than nothing.

Sleeping with Jack became the consolation prize. I didn't want a relationship with him. He was a fucking mess. I took in the taste of cigarettes and cheap beer when he kissed me, and I took in his careless cock when he wasn't too drunk to get it up. He lived in a sad, empty house; his wedding photos turned down on the bookshelf because he was too depressed and wasted to pack them away. The divorce papers weren't final but there were holes around the house where furniture ought to go and the refrigerator held nothing but beer and lunch meat. The paperwork was a mere formality at that point.

One morning, after a night of drunken antics, I woke up in Jack's king size bed. Tucked under the covers in my pajamas, I had fallen asleep long before Jack and his buddies wound down from the night. I remembered them bursting into the room and waking me up wrestling on and around the bed. Jack and his roommate had eventually passed out on either side of me, fully clothed on top of the blankets. James was asleep on the floor at the foot of the bed with his boots still on.

I didn't wake because of the sun streaming through the windows or the alarm going off for work, I woke because Jack's wife was standing over the bed screaming. I blinked open my bleary eyes and squinted at her. I had never seen this woman in my life. Or I should say, I had once seen a photo of this woman—but more beautiful, in a wedding gown with a thick layer of makeup and perfectly coiffed hair. The woman standing before me was something else entirely. She wore stained sweatpants and a messy bun and held the hand of a bawling toddler. Her face contorted with a rage that didn't quite compute in my half sleeping brain.

"Who the fuck are you? And why are you in my husband's bed?"

My mouth hung open and my brain fumbled desperately to assemble an appropriate response to such an assault.

"What are you? Some kind of whore? Are you sleeping with all three of them?" She looked around at what was obviously not the scene of a recent orgy.

"This is my fucking house and my fucking bed. And I bring my son in here to see his father and what does he see? Some other woman in my bed! What is he going to think?" she seethed.

If I were to hazard a guess as to what a three-year-old might think about people in a bed, with only a three-year-old's understanding of life and the purpose of beds, maybe, "look, people are sleeping"?

"You better get out of my house right now!" she yelled as she stormed out of the room with the whimpering child.

I let out a sigh of relief that she hadn't tried to fight me. James sat up from a dead sleep on the floor.

"That bitch is crazy," he said.

"You were awake the whole time?" I exclaimed. "And you just laid there pretending to sleep and didn't help me out?"

He winked.

I only saw Jack once more. I recognized I was better off alone than in a volatile situation where I didn't know who I could trust and who I might be subjected to. I stopped searching for love—I had learned my lesson.

Men only wanted one thing. It was something my father had told me throughout my teenage years. He had meant to scare me into chastity, I'm sure, but he hadn't accounted for my desires. I also only wanted one thing—to be loved. And if men only wanted one thing, and I only want one thing, then it seemed like we could work out a trade. Logically, to me, the one thing they wanted was a tool, to be used in my quest for the one thing I wanted.

Give them what they want. Then they will want you. Or so I had thought. But apparently it wasn't so simple. Or maybe the one thing I had to give just wasn't good enough?

Day 1: August 2, 2018
Mowich Lake → Golden Lakes

EVEN WITH AN EARLY BEDTIME, THE SUN RISES BEFORE I DO. MY PURPLE wool base layer top and baggy black leggings are almost too warm already. Walking to the pit toilets I am reconnected with the hiker-trash version of myself who last wore these leggings as camp pants—sitting on any number of rough natural surfaces, causing the large holes that now riddle the backside. My nervous energy bubbles over because I don't know what to expect for my first day on the trail, other than about ten miles.

When I refer to my Wilderness Trip Planner Map, I notice how little detail it contains. There is a list of elevations provided for each of the backcountry camps, except my starting point, Mowich Lake. A little less than four miles from here I'll be passing South Mowich River Camp (2,605 ft), and from there it's almost seven miles to Golden Lakes Camp (5,130 ft) where I'll stay tonight. Surely the hike to South Mowich River will be mostly downhill but I don't know how much, and a 2,500 ft climb in seven miles sounds pretty leisurely, so I give myself a little pep talk.

"Ten easy miles," I tell myself. "No big deal. You got this; you've done bigger miles before."

"Not in an awfully long time you haven't," the little doubting voice in my head snaps back. "Not with this pack on, not ten miles."

Packing my backpack goes quickly: sleeping bag and mat in the bottom, stuff sack full of clothes next, stove and food bag right on top. I roll up my tent and strap it to the outside of the pack. Even though I'm years out of practice, the routine is efficient.

I set off down the trail, trekking poles clacking merrily. Sounds of the car campers only now starting to light their stoves for coffee fall away immediately upon plunging into the greenery. Streams trickle from the side of the mountain over boulders coated in layers of nearly neon green moss. At regular intervals, I stop to take photos even though I know they will never capture the sensory experience. I can't photograph the burbling sound of moving water or the dewy smell of damp foliage. Perhaps some can photograph the way the light comes through the canopy in clearly visible beams, but I'm not much of a photographer, so I can't. It's the kind of place that sparkles in the morning light and I get the feeling I could have seen the fairies dancing, if only I had hit the trail a bit earlier.

What began as a gentle downhill grade steepens and transforms into a series of aggressive switchbacks. My pack is bumping up and down on my shoulders. I stop to adjust. A few steps later it's shifting from side to side, rubbing my hips. I stop to adjust again. I learned early on the Appalachian Trail not to overlook these adjustments. Three or four annoying stops to tighten and loosen my straps will help avoid serious chafing over the course of the day.

The sound of rushing water becomes discernible as I approach South Mowich River Camp. It's hard not to think of it as the halfway point for the day, even though I know it's not. It is still the first milestone of my journey. I have made it successfully from the beginning to somewhere else!

To my relief, the campsites here aren't gravel pads like Mowich Lake but flattened dirt areas—much easier for driving in tent stakes and hopefully an indication of what is to come. The camp is without a trail log. I'm disappointed, it would have been a nice excuse to stop a while and read. With more than six uphill miles still ahead of me, I redress my pack and keep moving.

———

The distinct dirt path I've been walking all morning disappears as I'm suddenly dumped out of the forest onto the rocky banks of South Mowich River. Milky water surges over and between large boulders, and it's easy to imagine the *thud thud thudding* of rocks moving downstream in the glacial flow like the ranger had described. Fallen logs are scattered throughout the rocks above and below where I stand. Several appear to have handrails attached. These bridges are obviously out of commission and strewn haphazardly in and out of the water. It takes some searching to find one that looks to be intentionally placed. I pick my way toward the bridge—a generous use of the term—balancing on rocks of all sizes while trying to keep my feet dry.

The bridge is a downed tree sliced lengthwise, so a flat surface is available for walking. The grooves that have been gouged into the face of the log for traction don't calm my nerves as I step one foot and then the other over the rushing water. My knuckles shine white as I grip the handrail with one hand while my trekking poles dangle from the opposite wrist. With each step, I look up and down the river, imagining the force of the water on my legs, lungs, and head. When I reach the other side of the bridge, I expel a lungful of stale air and look back over my shoulder. I remember the ranger's warning and wonder how many of these river crossings are in my future.

Standing halfway across the rocky wash between the wall of trees I emerged from and the one I am presumably headed into; I search for the trail. There doesn't seem to be another bridge, although there is another fork of the river to cross— admittedly much less terrifying than the one I've just faced. In my infinite wisdom I start toward the trees opposite, figuring the trail will make itself known to me as I approach. It's not long before I'm turning this way and that, trying to find a path of least resistance through the boulder field.

"Okay… somebody come rescue me…" I look desperately around.

I've only seen one person today. The trail is considerably less populated than I'm accustomed to, and normally I would appreciate the solitude. That's why I came out here alone, isn't it? I search up and down the river for any clue. My eyes land upon a cairn and my stress instantly dissipates. The tower of small rocks is balanced on a boulder about a hundred yards away.

Looking around, I spot several more rock pillars, strategically placed to mark the path down river from the bridge I crossed and not at all in the direction I've been walking. Cairns are often used to mark a hiking trail when the path is less than obvious—as in a boulder field or rocky riverbeds.

I cut a path toward the cairn and by the time I reach it

my little detour has amounted to about fifteen minutes of lost time. The designated path over the second fork of the river is a breeze and the woods envelope me once more. I say thanks to those who came before, establishing the trails I walk and marking them for others to follow. A trek like this would not be possible for someone like me without a trail. I may be ready to step out into my personal unknown, the true unknown is far greater than me.

———

The trail promptly begins to gain elevation and sweat beads on my brow. I huff and puff through the ascent and barely notice a thin layer of misty fog materializing. I've been hiking for years and it never seems to get easier. Negativity bounces around the inside of my skull.

This is so hard. Why is my backpack so heavy? Should I stop and take off my long sleeve? Who put this hill here? What have I gotten myself into? Why did I want to hike the Wonderland Trail again? Do I even like backpacking? I could turn back... I'd have to go up the huge hill I just came down. Good thing I went down before going up. How am I so out of shape?

Before reaching Golden Lakes the trail levels off, and a break in the trees reveals a beautiful hillside speckled with wildflowers in at least a dozen different colors. Shades of orange, pink, purple, and yellow wink back through the misty air. Their vibrancy is somehow simultaneously muted and intensified by the fog. I stand on the trail for several moments taking in the variety of flowers and the way the mist hangs in the air. I notice the water droplets clinging to leaves like morning dew, even though it's well past noon.

A mile or so later, the next clearing reveals the Golden Lakes Ranger Station, tucked among a cluster of trees with a small meadow laid out in front like the lawn of a house. It's the kind of scene you might imagine if you fantasize about running away to a cabin in the woods where nobody will ever bother you. Behind the cabin, fog rolls eerily around the still surface of the lake, dipping and twirling in a silent ballet. But seriously, it better not be all fucking gray and shitty for twelve days.

Assigned the group site, I follow a sign pointing left. After setting up my tiny tent in the corner of a space designed to hold six to twelve hikers, I change out of my damp wool shirt and into my dry fleece jacket. The mist continues to hang coolly in the air. Hopefully, my shirt will have a chance to dry before I need it again.

Several hours lazily creep by in silence as I gather water, make oatmeal for dinner, and stare into the lake. I crawl into my tent for warmth, but there's nothing going on there. Eventually, I head down to the Ranger Station. I find the trail log on the little wooden porch near a pair of abandoned pink long johns. Browsing through the pages, I find it hardly more satisfying than the one at Mowich Lake. My nearly getting lost at the river and several hours of alone time here at camp culminates in the following entry:

Dear Diary,
Got an early start this morning and skipped downhill from Mowich Lake. Crossed S Mowich River and had a snack. Yeesh, these river crossings are no joke! Climbed up a way and landed here. There is an eerie fog over the lake, which is breathtaking and makes me wonder where the occupants of the 5 other campsites are. I suppose they're making BIG MILES! and have further to come than I do.

I am taking my time on this journey, pondering the meaning of life, and daydreaming about meeting my true love in the wilderness. See you on the other side.

Best Day Ever!

-Lady Unicorn

Even though I vehemently despise nicknames, there is safety in the anonymity of my trail name. Lady Unicorn was foisted upon me on the Appalachian Trail after an aggressive round of twenty questions determined I "liked unicorns" and would not under any circumstance answer to the name Unicorn Girl. But I quickly became one with Lady Unicorn. She was my second identity, an alter ego with which I could depart from Christine's fears and traumas. And today Lady Unicorn can state her desire to find true love—Christine would never do that.

———

Not long after I return to my tent the sounds of hikers drift down the hill. A man comes from a trail I haven't yet explored and asks if this is the group site. He immediately turns back the other way upon confirmation. The stunted exchange leaves me with an anxious feeling; twelve days in the wilderness keeping to myself and having interactions like that one sounds lonely. I immediately question whether I am seeking solitude or some other form of independence.

Following the sound of the man's voice through the trees, I find that the trail creates a loop with some of the individual campsites. The man is in the second site with his hiking partner—another man. I approach sheepishly. Miles from the closest road, I'm not nervous they might be murderers as much as I'm concerned that I might look like a loser. Both men are around my age, both relatively attractive.

I'm flooded with regret about my slow pace and the lack of companionship I will find on my schedule. I didn't come out here to meet cute guys. I came out here to enjoy nature, which is exactly why I planned to go so slow on this trip.

"Hey, I heard sites four and five are where it's at, thought I'd come take a look," I say, as explanation for appearing uninvited in their campsite.

Thanks for the pro-tips, Trail Log.

"Oh yeah, that's what we heard too. Can't see much of anything with this fog, though. I think there's supposed to be a great view out this way." One of the men looks up from where he's pitching his tent and gestures vaguely at the misty, white expanse opposite the trail.

"Hmm." I stall, searching for something else to say, hands shoved awkwardly in the pockets of my purple fleece jacket. "Where are you guys coming from today?"

"Mowich Lake," he says.

"Oh, me too! Did you camp there?" I ask, a little too enthusiastically.

"No, we started hiking today, got kind of a late start," he explains.

"Today is my first day too. How many days are you hiking?" I ask.

"Nine." He doesn't look up.

We are both already bored with this conversation.

"Rad, I'm doing the twelve-day leisure schedule—taking my time." I search for some way to make a graceful exit, and quickly.

"Where are you headed tomorrow?" he asks.

"Only to North Puyallup, it's a short day." My face flushes with embarrassment at what now seems like a ridiculous itinerary.

"Oh yeah, that's only five miles isn't it? We're going to... South Puyallup, I think." They both nod their heads in confirmation. They're definitely leaving me in the dust tomorrow.

"Welp, I'll leave you guys to it."

The voices of social anxiety clang around my head as I walk away.

Does that count as a meaningful conversation? It must get easier. It definitely couldn't get any worse. Those guys are going to talk about the weird girl they met the first night of their thru-hike when they're old and gray.

Okay, no they won't.

I take a deep breath as I get back into my tent and mentally repeat a well-used mantra. *Nobody thinks about you as much as you think they do.* This brings me comfort in times of social distress and insecurity. It was silly to think I could seek out a meaningful connection per day without some forced small talk and the occasional finger guns while backing slowly out of the metaphorical room.

———

Back in my tent, I'm looking over my map when another much louder group pulls into the previously empty site directly above mine. Their thick European accents cut the air as they debate how to situate their tents and who will start cooking dinner.

"You are such a large group," one of the women says to me as she passes through. She nods to my overly spacious campsite and smiles sarcastically.

"Yeah, just me!" I put on my most cheerful voice.

"Can I ask you something?" Her face scrunches.

"Sure," I agree.

"Why are you alone?" Her voice is more demanding than

curious. The question is like a slap in the face, unexpected and stinging.

If I could answer that question, maybe I wouldn't be out here at all. At first, I was alone to prove that I was capable. To prove that I wasn't afraid to be alone. At some points, I have felt like I didn't have any other choice. I've experienced devastating rejection and loss. In response to nobody wanting me, I told myself I didn't want them either. I convinced myself I'd be better off alone. I know the ease that comes with aloneness and I've found satisfaction in it. I had been asking myself the same question just before she came along and rubbed it in my face.

"Why not?" My cheer falters.

In the past, when faced with this line of questioning, I have always been ready with fiery indignation. Why shouldn't a woman hike alone? I'm strong and independent, and I don't need anyone's approval or assistance to live my life. But not today. The fire and indignation have been snuffed out. I am meek.

"Yes, yes 'why not?' you say. But really why?" She is haughty and impatient. I owe her a justification for my audacious existence in this place. Her rowdy group of friends are crammed into an individual campsite and I'm not adequately filling the space assigned to me.

"I wanted to hike the trail, and I didn't know anyone else who could come," I answer truthfully, but not fully.

"Hmm." She leaves in a huff to rejoin the party at site five.

———

The night sky is an ominous gray as the thick layer of mist lifts and lowers throughout the evening. From the porch of the ranger station, where I can't hear the neighbors carrying on, I watch the weather fanatically. A rugged rock formation rises sharply across the meadow, and as the mist turns to rain it becomes completely obscured, only to be revealed again an hour or so later.

By bedtime, it has rained several times and the night is much colder than I would like. With my arms wrapped tightly at my waist, I shiver despite my layers. I close my eyes to the twilight and imagine a warm arm wrapped around me. I picture Tate, who was the last to hold me, and then I think of those who came before. In my imagination I am being embraced by a shape shifting parade of men, all of whose arms I have taken comfort in my adult life. But in reality, the only arms that hold me are my own.

It must be at least ten o'clock when I crawl into my sleeping bag fully clothed. I have no intention of an early start for my five-mile downhill tomorrow. I'll wait out the rain if I can.

Chapter 2

When Taylor told me he loved me, I wasn't ready to say it back. I was afraid I wouldn't know real love when I found it. He looked into my eyes—really looked. He said I was beautiful, just because. He brought me lunch at work and left notes on my windshield. He was everything a girl could ask for, and *he* loved *me*. How could I possibly deserve him after everything I had done wrong? He was my chance at normal, at partnership, an escape from the revolving door of men that never wanted to call me theirs.

On a spring afternoon in 2010, we cruised down the highway in rural Arkansas, pointed toward Little Rock and our tiny apartment in the city. Taylor held my right hand from the passenger seat, idly twirling the ring on my finger as he often did in moments of silence. I had been wearing the platinum set diamond engagement ring since the age of thirteen. It was a family heirloom passed down on my father's side, a symbol of the love that led here. I could almost hear the blood throbbing laboriously through my body from the exertion of our two-mile walk. My fingers were swollen from the day's heat, so the ring didn't move as freely as it normally did on my long slender finger. I probably couldn't have taken it off if I tried.

I was grateful for the distraction of driving, at least that was something I could do well. This was a realm in which my body would not let me down in front of the man I loved. I could go as fast as I wanted without the betrayal of my red face and ragged breathing, or my heart pumping out of my chest and my knees growing weak with each step.

The same was not true on the trail. I had fooled Taylor, like I had been fooling myself for years. I was not overweight, so he thought I was healthy, capable; truthfully, I was soft and out of shape. I tried to keep up with his impossible pace, and each time he turned back to see where I had disappeared to, all the injustices of this body came crashing down on me. By the time we reached the car, tears streamed silently down my face.

I tried to explain—things were harder for me. They always had been. I couldn't breathe, my legs got tired so easily, my heart was working too hard—I was choking on it. He looked at me with mixed confusion and concern, as if he had never experienced any of these sensations. His response only verified my suspicion that this aspect of my being was wholly unfair.

"Maybe you should see a doctor?" he suggested gently.

"I don't think there's anything actually wrong with me. Everything is just... it's just hard." I reiterated the amorphousness of my complaint. It would have been so easy to hope I had some kind of medical explanation for my lack of physical capabilities, but could it be so simple? I longed to relinquish the shame of my body's failure. To be able to say it's not my fault.

"Well, we should hike more, it will get easier." His voice

was soft, almost pleading.

I glowered as the tears came again. The last thing I wanted was to put myself through the physical and emotional torture of another day like today.

"I don't know." I did know. He was right. A long silence hung in the air. I stared straight ahead, the yellow dashes on the road counting the seconds as we continued on. I had no excuse for the way my body behaved, and the idea of trying to explain it was like teaching someone a language I myself didn't know.

"I love you. And I care about you. I'm worried about you.... I'm worried you're going to end up like your mom," he whispered.

My eye twitched. I pulled my hand away from his and placed it on the steering wheel. Driving suddenly required all my physical attention as my mind raced. From the corner of my eye, I saw his hand come to rest lamely on his thigh. My throat constricted and my stomach turned. He had cut me with a knife of my own making, and I thought I might be sick.

I longed to come to my mother's defense, to fill the car with the sounds of her successes, to berate him for suggesting there was anything about her that I didn't desire to become. The voices raged in my head, but no words escaped. The quiet became oppressive, hanging thickly around us. My vision went blurry as my fingers tightened on the tacky hot steering wheel. I wished he would stop looking at me with those sad eyes.

My mind zoomed to the engagement ring tucked away in his dresser drawer. When he was at work, I often slid the white gold band onto my left ring finger and wore it around the house—admiring the center pearl with its tiny diamond accents on each side. We would be married at twenty and twenty-one, same as my parents. I had picked out the ring myself, same as my mom.

I remembered the wedding dress I had fallen in love with online and cried in at the bridal store. After weeks of imagining myself in the short flapper-style number, I had stood before the mirror in the dressing room staring at the beaded sheath stretched tightly over my hips and thighs and wondered why I didn't look like the waifish model in the photos online. My mother could see the disappointment on my face. She knew this style wasn't suited to my body, because my body was her body, less sixty pounds. The unmistakable likeness started with our height and extended to our thick, hairy legs. In that moment I was overcome by the betrayal of my own figure—all the ways it had failed me. Yet I had not reflected any of this blame on the woman before me, the one who made me in her own image.

When I looked at myself and thought, "Fat. Ugly. Unlovable." I always came away feeling angry at myself—never her. When I looked at her I saw a mother. She was large and soft and comfortable, like a mom should be.

I sifted through memories of my childhood. The matching outfits she sewed for us, along with a third tiny replica for my favorite doll. There was a sweet irony in the fact that I was the only one who ever outgrew mine, leaving her and my doll with identical jumpers. Standing on the kitchen table while she cut my long curly hair and sitting on the living room floor while she braided it into complicated plaits she had learned from a book. Snuggling into her soft body and studying the neat rows of stitches she produced while watching television, seeming never to look down at the fabric except during commercial breaks.

My mom struggled with her weight my whole life. She wasn't happy with her body, but she tried not to let me see. Still, by the age of seven or eight, I worried about my weight too and regularly asked her which of two foods was healthier. I was small for my age, but never athletic. Playing soccer during recess never crossed my mind. I even quickly became adamantly opposed to tag, having felt the burning embarrassment of being the only "It" who couldn't catch anyone. I had withdrawn from all physical activities, preferring to spend recesses in the classroom helping my teacher wipe down overhead projector sheets and earning brownie points. I performed as required in PE with shame and tears. I felt as though something was wrong with me my whole life, and after high school I had been allowed a reprieve from mandatory physical pursuits.

I never directly attributed my failures to the genetics and habits of my mom, but I suppose to deny them was as unfair as it felt to accept them. Still, it didn't seem appropriate for Taylor to be the one to put words to my shameful fear. I loved my mom and to say I didn't want to end up like her felt like a betrayal, a secret I would take to the grave. I wouldn't blame her for my own shortcomings.

———

Taylor's pitying gaze haunted me, and his words rang in my ears. Only a few months later, I ended our relationship. I couldn't reconcile who I was in the world with his concern clinging to me like spiderwebs. I couldn't quite explain to Taylor or my parents why I walked away from the life we had planned. To back out on our future felt like a failing of epic proportions. None of them knew how deeply I saw myself through his eyes. The only man who had ever loved me had found a flaw.

I hadn't yet developed the clarity of mind to admit there were aspects of my mother I did not hope to inherit. My father had never found fault in my mother, and I had thought that Taylor saw me in the same way. To marry Taylor had been an attempt to bypass my own becoming and step directly into her shoes. Our marriage would have been the very reason I became the woman he feared to see in my future.

I moved back into my parents' house in the suburbs of Little Rock within weeks of their move to Alaska. The Coast Guard had always told my dad where to go and this time, I wasn't coming with. I was halfway through college, and we all agreed it would be best for me to stay put and finish my degree.

With my parents 3,000 miles away, my freedom felt dark and infinite. My rebellions never seemed big enough without anyone around to witness the damage. Like a toddler testing limits, I pushed and pushed but now there were no parents to tell me when I had crossed the line. At twenty years old I wasn't ready to establish my own boundaries, so I lived without them. I accepted all behaviors—from myself and everyone around me.

A few select bars in Little Rock never questioned my fake ID. I was thirty-seven years old and 5'7". One of them was a dueling piano bar where I could sing my heartache away, belting out "Sweet Caroline" and "Living on a Prayer" at the top of my lungs with a bottom shelf vodka cranberry in my hand. I didn't know what not turning into my mom looked like but drowning my loneliness and social ineptitude in cheap booze seemed like a good start. On nights when I couldn't find a friendly guy to take me in, I would drive the bright, empty interstate back to my parents' empty house, trusting my internal autopilot and fate to get me home alive.

It was hard to discern on any given night whether it was more dangerous to drink and drive or to go home with any man who would have me. Most of the time, I crawled into a foreign bed next to some Devin or Spencer or Michael and passed out without so much as a goodnight kiss. The alcohol coursed through my veins and I slept like the dead.

I drank to blackout over and over again—putting myself in ever more precarious positions. Maybe if I could drink enough and wake up unscathed enough times, I could undo that one night. I was searching for redemption from the night I had found myself lying on the bathroom floor. Trying to convince myself that it didn't have to end that way. Or maybe just begging to forget it altogether.

At my six a.m. alarm, I would dig through the clothes in my car to find something halfway presentable and head straight to work. Sitting at my desk, I stared into the abyss of the computer's dull glow. I nibbled saltines and sipped water as cycles of nausea pulsed through me. Inevitably, I would text my girlfriends to see where they had ended up at the end of the night and what time they were free to meet up after work. We exchanged stories of escapades, compared dick sizes, and laughed about losing our shoes and our dignity. Being a mess is funny as long as you're in it together.

I never asked what they were trying to forget.

———

Not long after my twenty-first birthday, the legality of my consumption made it that much easier. One night, I went out dancing with a coworker; I knew he was interested in me and I flirted enough to get free drinks out of the deal. He kept them coming, and we danced late into the night in a way that could only be described as sexual. He took me back to his apartment where my car was parked but I was in no state to drive. He insisted I stay because it wouldn't be safe to leave.

He stooped so I could lean on his shoulder to get up the stairs and into his bed. I immediately rolled over and closed my eyes. I must have been alone in the bed for only a few minutes but was nearly asleep when I felt his hands suddenly at my waist. He rubbed my back and slid his hands under my shirt. It felt like a dream—the kind of dream where you want to run or scream but are frozen in place. My brain shouted: *Stop! Don't! I'm leaving*. But my mouth said nothing, and my eyes remained closed in the darkness. As he stripped my clothes off, I tried helplessly to lift my arms from the bed, to push him away, but they were too heavy—immobilized by long island iced teas.

There was a still silence in the room, only the sound of skin on skin and his steady breathing broke the air. The familiar smell of rubber and lubricant filled my nostrils. Through the fog I thought, at least he's using a condom.

When he was done with me, he rolled over and fell asleep. I did too. The next day, I awoke with a cloudy brain and a pit in my stomach. I had led him on, I had gone out with him, I had gotten too drunk to drive. I hadn't said no because I couldn't find that one little syllable—many infants' first word—it had eluded me.

When I told a friend about the incident, they suggested that I had put myself in an obvious position and I could hardly blame the guy for what he did. I didn't cry. After all, I could hardly blame the guy.

———

That wasn't the day I decided to give up drinking. As a matter of fact, I was only getting started. It was easy to pretend alcohol was doing me a service. It is, after all, a great "social lubricant." Every shot of tequila allowed me to put myself out there in a way I would never have the confidence to sober. But it was also making me into a person I would never have been sober. I was funny and loud and forward, I flirted with men I considered way out of my league. But the Christine they met wasn't the real one, she had gone into hiding a long time ago.

When I met Nick at a bar, he told me he wasn't in the Air Force, even though he and his friends were all smooth faced and clean cut. When I went home with him and saw his flight suit hanging in the closet, I ribbed him for the lie. He confessed. The next time we were together, I pointed out the name on his driver's license wasn't Nick or Nicholas or Nicolai, but Tarsus. He confessed again. I continued to call him Nick. It wasn't long before we were taking shots and two-stepping the nights away with his buddies. I knew he was telling them it wasn't serious. How could it be? We were never ourselves with each other.

A few weeks before my college graduation we went to Greers Ferry Lake, famed for its cliff jumping. A long craggy rock outcrop rises out of the water to a height of around forty feet. Arkansans spend summer days jumping off and clamoring back to the top of the wall to jump off again in droves. In the midst of military bravado and mass consumption of Coors Light, the testosterone was running high. I stood at the top of the forty-foot cliff looking down. The guys fake shoved each other and howled as they stumbled back from the edge.

"Are you going to jump?" Nick looked at me with "double-dog dare" written all over his face.

"Of course!" I smiled wryly and took a long pull from a handle of vodka. My stomach flip-flopped and I swallowed hard. I knew I didn't have any business cliff-jumping. The spinal surgery I'd had years before left me with a long list of doctor-prescribed "don'ts" which included jumping, horseback riding and skiing. There was nothing appealing about the precipitous drop and my own daring would never have pushed me over the edge. But I had something to prove to these guys—I was cool, I could hang, I was the kind of girl who knew how to have a good time.

I ran the short approach to the edge of the rock and flung myself off. Not quite knowing how to manage my body during the seconds of free fall, I flailed my limbs and managed not to scream. When my body broke the surface of the water, it felt more like slamming into a brick wall than anything I had ever experienced.

The shock of the impact forced the air from my lungs and a large bubble floated away from me. My mind reeled, but the oxygen deprivation quickly silenced all thoughts but one. I was going to be paralyzed, all to jump off a dumb cliff into a dumb lake with some dumb guys I didn't even care about.

I managed to reach the surface, not sure if by my own volition or by physical buoyancy. The rasping choking noise that escaped my gasping mouth was the most horrific sound I had ever heard, let alone produced. I desperately searched around for help. Somebody floated toward me with an inner tube and as soon as it was within reach, I clung to it for my life. The pain surged through my body as if it were in my veins although I couldn't pinpoint its source. While it registered that I was not dead or paralyzed, I was sure I wouldn't walk away from this without serious repercussions.

I stayed in the water for more than twenty minutes after the jump, holding on to the inner tube and trying not to move my body. With each long shallow breath, I took care not to expand my lungs too far. The guys asked if I was alright, more out of concern for the rest of their day than for me. When I was finally ready to get out of the water, Nick helped me climb the rock face back to the point I had jumped from. Every step was excruciating so I found a place where I could lie down on the stone slab and not bother anybody.

I closed my eyes to the blinding sun and watched the bright red insides of my eyelids.

"Just breathe. Slow. In. Out. Everything is going to be fine. Just breathe through it," I whispered to myself.

Strangers walked around me as if I were a feature in the rock. People continued to jump from the cliffs, whooping and screaming. My companions continued to revel and enjoy a perfect Saturday at the lake.

Just breathe.

I inhaled slowly, taking in as much air as my lungs would allow without expanding my rib cage. I pushed each breath out between pursed lips with my arms wrapped firmly around my abdomen, holding everything in place. My back muscles had seized tightly around my spine and every movement caused shooting pain in my entire body.

I lay on the ground, hugging myself and holding back tears, wondering if I would forever be downplaying my own pain for the comfort of those around me.

In the weeks that followed, I begged my spine to heal, cringing through every movement. To visit a doctor, to have my injury evaluated, would make it real. If I could just ignore it long enough, I would be whole again.

I couldn't explain myself to my parents. My bad choices and self-destructive behavior were piled so high that to explain what was going on in my life would have required the spinning of a web of lies so complex as to be impossible to remember.

"Who were you with?" they would ask.

I couldn't possibly tell them the real name of the guy I was with. Or the fake one. Or that he was in the military. My dad would love that almost as much as he would love the idea that I somehow thought cliff-jumping was safe or appropriate for somebody with a fused spine. It was stupid. I knew it was stupid.

As I struggled through my painful mistakes without the support of my parents, my aloneness became ingrained. I had wonderful loving parents who had done their best to teach me wrong from right. They had stressed the importance of education and independence. They had given me the basic tools for success and a constant barrage of warnings about the dangers of the world. But there I was, deep in the trenches of inexcusable mistakes and shameful behavior, with nobody to turn to. I couldn't let them see me like this.

But then they came home from Alaska earlier than expected. When they moved back, I was supposed to move out. But I'd blown all my money and quit my job. I was somehow five years in and still making my way through a bachelor's degree.

My mom pressed her lips tightly together when she saw the state of the house. I hadn't vacuumed the carpets in months—why would I? I almost never came home. The four bedrooms, kitchen, dining room, and living room were too much for one person. Too much empty space, space that had once been filled with family.

We cleaned together before my dad came back, his work in Alaska not quite done. We unpacked their things when the moving truck arrived. Mom told me I could stay until graduation, but then I must move out. I had a little less than a year. I didn't want to be there anyway—too close to her. Where she might smell the menthol cigarettes I'd taken to smoking or ask me where I'd been for the last three days. My mistakes had grown too big, too outrageous to explain away now with her so close.

Day 2: August 3, 2018

Golden Lakes → North Puyallup River

MY NOISY NEIGHBORS ARE USING MY CAMPSITE AS A THOROUGHFARE —I don't mind. They are out in the lightly falling rain trying to start their day, and I'm still comfortably tucked in bed. My map crinkles and rustles as I review the plan for the day. North Puyallup River camp (3,750 ft) is exactly five miles from Golden Lakes camp (5,130 ft). It's unlikely the next five miles will be a meandering descent of less than 1,500 feet, so I mentally prepare for anything. Anything except five miles in the rain. Surely this will clear before noon and I can get going with the sun at my back.

The morning hours pass slowly as I drift in and out of sleep. I listen as my neighbors pack up and hit the trail. The rain ought to let up but sprinkles consistently patter on my rainfly as hours slip by. I toss and turn in my tent waiting for the glow of the sun. The cocoon of my sleeping bag is silky and damp with moisture collected through the night. My limbs are warm but confined within it. I struggle to feel free without letting cold air in around my neck.

Finally, it must be near noon and I think if I get moving

the rain might stop in time for me to pack up. The drizzling continues without improvement while I cook and eat ramen for breakfast. I do my best to pack my things without getting too much water in my backpack. The precipitation could be a function of the elevation, and once I start downhill it may stop.

As I pass by the ranger station on the way back to the trail, I see new faces. Two men and a woman, all at least in their fifties, decked out in full rain gear are clearly searching for a dry place to shed the moisture they have collected on their way in.

"Hello," I say, waving as I approach.

"Hello," one of the men greets me in a fatherly tone, "where are you headed? We are going counter-clockwise to North Puyallup."

"I'm going to North Puyallup too," I say. "Do you know what the trail looks like between here and there? I only have the trip planning map and it doesn't really have an elevation profile." I guess this group must have a real map—old school trail convention requires it.

"Yeah, so there's a bit more to climb from here, maybe a few hundred feet, and then it's all downhill from there," the man offers brightly. "You are welcome to take a look at our map."

"That would be great." My curiosity gets the best of me. Hiking without an elevation profile frees my mind from the ongoing sense of dread that comes with a list of ascents and little four-digit numbers. So, I only look at the trail details for today. It's just as he said, a few hundred more feet of climbing and it's all downhill from there.

Leaving the party to their lunch, I head off up the trail, hoping to put a bit of distance between us and avoid hours of leapfrogging. The rain coming down is almost pleasant on the uphill climb, keeping me cool but not too wet. The trail is another story. The dirt path cuts through sections of knee-high growth that don't appear to be actively managed in any way. Bushes and tall grasses lean over the trail from both sides. It's impossible to move along without brushing the leaves and soaking my legs from the water collected in the plants.

The uphill climb is short-lived, and I'm headed back down within the hour. I stop occasionally to take in the surroundings. Although the epic views are obscured, the mist has a beauty of its own. As I suspected, the cloud cover begins to lift as I descend toward the river. The tips of my toes jam repeatedly toward the front of my shoes with each downward step. I don't want to stop and look at them, for fear that I've broken skin. My knees grow tired from the rhythmic impact. I sympathize with people who say hiking down is harder than hiking up, although I still don't agree with them.

Hundreds of bushes along the trail are littered with what look like blueberries. I don't know my wild berries well enough to know whether these are safe to eat or if there exists an insidious blueberry look-alike to be wary of. Pausing to study the bushes, I note that there seem to be two different kinds of berries which appear nearly identical. On closer inspection, one goes through a reddish plum phase on its way to ripe and the other more of a true blue.

I decide to risk my life and try one. Human instincts should tell me if it's poison, plus they are so tiny, it couldn't kill me if I only eat one. I pop one of the bluer ones in my mouth. It tastes like a berry—kind of sour. Could be an under-ripe blueberry. Shrugging to myself, I eat a couple more. I'm not far from camp now so shouldn't have time to die before I arrive.

The telltale sounds of rushing water reach up to me as I approach North Puyallup River camp. From the north, I enter the individual campsites first and see a sign pointing further along the trail, toward the group site and toilet. Three individual sites are nestled among the trees in a neat row, far enough above the river that it's out of sight. I choose the middle site because it seems driest after the rain. The ground is hard, and I struggle to bury my tent stakes. As soon as I get one side of the tent erected, the other collapses again. I stomp back and forth, shoving the stakes into the ground with increased vigor each time. After my fourth attempt to secure the foot box, I stand up and swear to myself. In a huff, I collect the stakes back into the tiny nylon bag from whence they came and pick up my half-assembled tent. Shelter in hand, I march down the path to the first site and find the slightly wetter surface more agreeable.

I proceed with blowing up my sleeping mat, unpacking my pack, and changing into my camp clothes. Upon removing my shoe, I grimace at a quarter-sized blister on the pad of my big toe. The white distended pocket is puffy and tender to the touch. I slip into my camp shoes, a light pair of purple sandals with Velcro straps. Hopefully getting my feet out of my damp shoes and socks will keep the blister at bay until I can find a bandage.

The only first aid supply I possess is three Benadryl tablets. It looks like I'm going to have to rely on the kindness of strangers for this one.

———

Grabbing my water filter and empty bottle, I head through the group campsite to the water source. The trail leads steeply downhill and winds through more dense, wet berry bushes. My sandals are an inappropriate choice for the walk, and they cause me to slip and slide in the muck. I make it safely to the bridge crossing over North Puyallup River, which isn't anything like the bridge I tiptoed over at South Mowich River; it's strong and sturdy and appears to have been standing for quite some time. It isn't balanced precariously on the boulders that make up the bank of the river but planted firmly in the trail on either side of the river which plummets more than fifty feet directly beneath the bridge. The crashing chaos of the surging water is the only sound I can hear when crossing. The foaming, hissing, splashing is mesmerizing to watch, and the carved-out rock wall being slowly eaten away by the continuous force is a testament to the power of motion.

I kick myself for not bringing my book down with me—to sit in my campsite hidden from this view would be silly. Past the river lies the group campsite, quite separated from the rest of us up the hill. Then there are two open air privies— nothing but a toilet seat atop a collection container with one wall attempting, unsuccessfully, to hide the user from view of the trail. The presence of privies on popular long trails, no matter how silly or public they may be, protect the beautiful places we are all out here to enjoy. Even a well-used and far from civilized toilet is a vastly superior experience than finding human poop on a trail or near a campsite.

Signs indicate a water source further along the trail, so I continue past the toilets to see what all the fuss is about. I've already passed a half dozen spots between the individual camps and the bridge where water could be easily collected. Perhaps during drier seasons those trickles are non-existent. At intervals between the heavy brush I can see where people or animals have pushed through to a stream burbling off to the left of the trail. One particular opening seems well-traveled, so I pick my way through the bushes. There are large, smooth river rocks in the stream, and I balance on one while scooping up water.

Once I've filled my two containers, I rise from a crouch and promptly slip off the slick stone I've been squatting on. My right foot slides ankle-deep into the cold water, and the stone dislodges and rolls over the top of my foot. The shock of the cold and the pain of the blunt force land simultaneously on my nerves and I nearly topple over. With a water vessel in each hand, I manage to steady myself on my left foot and yank my right from under the rock.

If you slip and crush your foot in the forest and there is nobody there to witness, is it still embarrassing? All jokes aside, the risk of injury far from a trailhead is a real one. This trail is popular enough that I wouldn't perish alone with a broken ankle, though rescuing me would probably ruin someone's day.

I take a moment to compose myself before wrestling my way back through the bushes to the trail. When I get back to the group campsite, I find the threesome from earlier setting up camp.

"Hey, how was your hike?" I inquire, though I imagine it was much the same as mine, just thirty minutes later.

"Good! It's a beautiful day, we are ready to get dry clothes on though. Did you find the water source?" One man points to my containers.

"Yeah, it's not far at all, but I had to dive through the bushes a bit to get to it." I leave out the part about nearly falling in the stream. "I was actually hoping to catch you over here, I developed a pretty big blister today and I don't have any supplies for it. I've never gotten a blister hiking before, so I'm totally unprepared," I explain.

I know people with first aid kits love to be the hero, but I still feel awkward asking for help from strangers.

"Robert's the one with the feet supplies, I'm sure he can set you up," the man offers.

I look over to Robert and he appears delighted to be able to provide feet supplies.

Robert produces an extensive selection of blister bandages of all shapes and sizes and insists I take a few for later. I find a large, thick, oval one with a jelly-like consistency and wrap it from the bottom of my toe up around the sides. It's incredibly sticky and covers the area well. I thank them for doctoring me up and head back to my camp.

―――――

With the lay of the land and an added protective layer on my toe, I make my way back over the river and up the hill. When I get back to my tent, I see that someone else has made it to camp. He walks between sites two and three, and I can tell on first glance he's an ultra-lighter, a class apart from regular thru-hikers and my secret envy. I consider myself to be a savvy packer and categorically minimalist, but my Osprey Aura might as well be a leather suitcase compared to his super-techy Hyperlite cuben fiber number.

Since my time on the AT there have been significant advancements in ultra-light technology. The gear continues to get fancier and more expensive, but the philosophy remains the same: trade camping comfort for hiking comfort. In exchange for sometimes being cold, and sometimes wet, and sometimes without, you can hike with ease and a base weight well below twenty pounds. Too good to be true? Depends on which comforts you prioritize. I'm in the warm and dry club and have been hesitant to relinquish my membership, but I have definitely stood by enviously as ultra-lighters breezed by me on the trail.

My current return to backpacking has prompted me to contemplate purchasing updated gear. I'm curious about his rig and his opinion on the balance of advantage and sacrifice. Instead of returning to the bridge, I hang around my tent pretending to be busy and give him some time to set up his camp before approaching. When he seems appropriately established, I wander over.

"Hey, I was starting to wonder if anybody else was going to show up," I open.

"Oh hi, yeah it's a pretty small camp, huh. I'm Adam."

He is shorter than me, dark hair, very thin. His clothes are the epitome of functional: an off-white long-sleeve technical button down and black running shorts. His floppy hat is the same one tourists buy in national parks when they are going on a one-mile hike and don't want to get sunburned. He might be the first person I have ever seen wearing one with any type of validity.

"Hi. I'm Christine." I smile. "I've been here for hours by myself, where'd you come from today?"

"I started at Mowich Lake, you?" he asks.

"I only came from Golden Lakes today, I started at Mowich Lake yesterday." I tell him.

"How was camping at Golden Lakes? It looked really nice." He looks up at me with the eagerness of a child and I can't ignore his boyish good looks.

"Beautiful!" I say. "It was foggy all night, and it rained off and on. I'm sure the lake would have been lovely on a clear day."

"Definitely! The water was nice and warm when I stopped,

I should have stayed for a swim," he laments.

"Totally! I'm hoping we have more sunny days coming. I didn't check the weather before I left, and I don't know if I'm prepared for twelve days of rain," I say.

"You're hiking for twelve days? That's awesome, savoring it. I'm only doing six." His smile seems completely devoid of judgmental subtext.

"Wow, six days! You're gonna leave me in the dust. Where are you headed tomorrow?" I ask.

"Devil's Dream." Adam grimaces.

"Me too! I've heard it's awful." I put on my comical fake frown to cover my excitement at having a two-day friend.

"Yeah, that's what everybody is saying. The bugs are supposed to be the worst there," he says.

"It's my longest hiking day of the trip, so I figure I'll probably get into camp pretty late anyway. There's some place right before called Indian Henry's. We could stop and hang out there for a bit and head to Devil's Dream just in time to jump in our tents and call it a night," I suggest.

I look at his shelter and in true ultra-light fashion, it's hardly useful protection from blood-thirsty swarms of mosquitoes and black flies. What is unmistakably a green poncho is held up by one trekking pole. The outstretched body is staked down in every direction creating a sort of teepee-like structure with a hood flopping uselessly at the top. The bottom of the poncho doesn't reach the ground and his sleeping pad can easily be seen in the inches of open space.

"Well, if it's too awful, you could always crash in my tent," I offer.

"That might be nice. This ultra-light rig is great, but the bugs can definitely get in," he admits.

We debate the merits of several ultra-light strategies, and he is cracking me up with some of his insights. Such gems as: "I like to wear tall socks, because you can use the extra fabric at the top as a towel if something gets wet" and "I prefer cold oatmeal." As it turns out, his minimalist style is not limited to backpacking—he has a full-time job and lives in a Ford Fiesta in Portland. I wonder if he eats cold oatmeal in real life too.

Soon the sun sets, and the evening is winding down. My cheeks are sore after several hours of hanging out by Adam's poncho tent.

"I should probably get to bed. What time do you normally get going in the morning?"

"I don't have a set time, but eight-ish maybe," he says.

"Could you yell at me if you're up getting ready and don't see me?"

"Definitely." Adam nods energetically.

"I've got plenty of room in my tent tonight too." I point to the open bottom of the poncho shelter.

"Okay, thanks," he says.

I crawl into bed alone, hoping he might follow, but fall asleep immediately.

Chapter 3

WHEN MY MOM WAS DIAGNOSED WITH BREAST CANCER, I WONDERED if she would want me to stay at home. But I didn't want to stay. Once the first rounds of chemotherapy started, she would often sit in the La-Z-Boy recliner watching TV, puking into a trash can at intervals. Whenever she started with the warning hiccups, I went immediately to my room and snapped the door shut.

She didn't lose her hair during the first round of chemotherapy, but when that course of toxins didn't knock out the cancer the doctors recommended another. When she came home with the news, she let the tears go.

"Nobody cares if you have hair," I told her, plopping down on the couch.

Her red face twisted in anguish. Oh no. I had said the wrong thing.

"Because we love you. And whether or not you have hair doesn't change that," I tried to console her.

"Okay," she sniffled. "Just promise you won't let me be that woman with only a few patches of hair left. When it starts to look bad, you have to tell me so we can cut it off."

"Promise." I looked into her eyes. "Do you want me to cut off my hair too?"

The look of horror on her face might have been comical if it wasn't for the tears.

"Why would I want you to do that? You have beautiful hair." She shook her head and I smiled, relieved.

It wasn't long before she was leaving five or ten hairs behind on the sofa at the end of the night. I silently plucked loose hairs from the back of her sweater as we walked through the mall. She confided in me that clumps were coming out in the shower, sliding down her body like little hairy creatures, making their escape and clogging the drain.

"Does it look bad? Can you tell?" she would ask.

"No, you can't really tell. You had so much hair to start with." I would assure her, even though the hair on one side of her head was significantly thicker than the other. Her scalp was not yet showing, and I thought that's what we were hoping to avoid.

She wanted me to shave her head so that my father wouldn't have to. But every time she asked, I would say "wait a little longer."

One day I came home from school to find my parents both sitting in the living room, staring stony faced at the TV. Mom was as bald as an egg. Dad's eyes were puffy and red. Heat rose in my stomach—I had failed her. She had wanted me to be there. To ceremoniously say goodbye to her hair, our most unifying feature. She had spent the better part of my first fifteen years grooming my hair—washing and brushing it, tying it up, curling and straightening it. I had missed my chance to repay her.

She took to brushing and braiding my hair again. I sat on my knees before her, twenty-two years old, feeling the tug of the comb against my scalp. She didn't speak of her grief, but I felt it in her fingers. My hair was hers. It was the closest thing she had left of the woman she had once been. My future was hers. I was the closest thing she had to the woman she had once planned to become. Before cancer made her question the woman she had time left in this world to be.

———

In fall of 2013, I sat in a gray cubicle in Little Rock, Arkansas, 4.3 miles from the modest two-bedroom apartment I shared with another recent college graduate. I clacked away on my keyboard and glanced back and forth between my dual monitors. The beep of my headset was the only warning that my ear was about to be filled with the questions and complaints of an insurance salesman in Tennessee. Between phone calls I shuffled papers and updated Excel spreadsheets, sometimes sneaking away from my desk to visit my mom's new office on the other side of the building.

The job was nothing interesting to me, but I completed tasks efficiently and found myself with more and more free time during the forty-hour work week. I spent entire days surfing the web, following link after link, and succumbing to click-bait at a time when it was nearing its clickiest. One day in August, I clicked on an article, *Inside the World's Most Dangerous Amusement Park.* Minutes later, I was immersed in a Wikipedia page devoted to New Jersey's famed Action Park which directly claimed no fewer than six lives in the 1980s.

Each time I escaped down one of these rabbit holes I became momentarily engrossed in the stories of others. I imagined myself, a child in the 1980s, whipping around the steep corners of a dangerous water slide only to be flung from the rim and rushed to the emergency room—a wicked grin on my tiny face, bursting with the thrill of it all.

In September, I found a hiking forum called White Blaze. In the years since my relationship with Taylor had ended the concept of hiking continued to elude me. It was something I wanted to want to do. I was ashamed to admit I found it quite miserable. Perhaps I just didn't understand the point. Perhaps these people on the internet could enlighten me. White Blaze was all about the Appalachian Trail, which I had never heard of, so there was a lot to learn.

Countless hours were spent reading about the best trekking poles for long distance, the best hostels on the trail, and how to avoid Norovirus. I steadfastly consumed tips on how best to dehydrate your own spaghetti sauce and perused the packing lists of first timers and ultra-lighters. The passion on the screen was impossible to turn away from. Hikers discussed what hiking meant to them and how they longed for the freedom of the trail. Each time I read about someone taking that first step, I was aflame. These people spoke of leaving behind dead end jobs, hopeless marriages, and destructive drug addictions. The trail didn't know who you were before you got there—it allowed for reinvention.

It was more than the mystery of the unknown and the freedom of the trail. It was about the forum itself, a place for hikers to come together and talk about hiking. The community was welcoming and focused. These people were *about* something. I wanted to be about something too.

I leapt up from my desk and marched into my mother's office.

"Hey, I'm going to hike the Appalachian Trail!" My cheeks were flushed with excitement and the vigorous one-minute walk. The crazed smile and wild announcement had to be a frightening thing for my mother to process.

"What?" Her mouth hung slightly open, nothing but confusion registering on her face.

"So, I've been reading about this trail, it goes from Georgia to Maine. It's two thousand one hundred and eighty-four miles, and you start in Georgia and walk and walk and walk until you get to Maine. Doesn't it sound great!" I stumbled over the words as they rushed out. It was as if I had known these facts my entire life and they were just waiting for the moment to pour out.

"What?" she repeated, blinking slowly.

I widened my eyes for emphasis. What else was there to say? How could anyone not see this was the greatest thing since sliced bread?

"No, it doesn't sound great, it sounds crazy. Why would you want to do that?" The sharpness of her tone was a pin in my enthusiasm—I deflated.

"Moooooom," I whined, pleading for her understanding—a big ask. "This is something I really want to do. Can you please be supportive?"

"Christine, this is just some new thing you heard about and think you want to do. You'll forget about it as soon as some other thing comes up. I'm not going to argue with you. It sounds dangerous and miserable, and I don't even understand why you think you want to do it. Come on." She raised her non-existent eyebrows.

"No, Mom. I want to do this, for real. Next year. I'm going to plan everything, you'll see." I glared defiantly, daring her to retract the one thousand times she had told me I could do anything I set my mind to. I strutted back to my desk and flopped into my chair. I would show her, I would show anyone who doubted me. Thru-hiking is not about physical fitness or experience, it's about finding yourself and following your dream. It's about proving yourself and redefining the parameters of life. It was all there on White Blaze—becoming a hiker isn't about enjoying a long walk up a mountain, rather the self-exploration you pursue along the way.

It was the first time I wanted to hike, and I wanted it bad. Thru-hiking the Appalachian Trail was suddenly synonymous with finding my own reason for being and proving I could, in fact, do whatever I set my mind to. I needed to know that I wasn't destined to remain the sedentary office worker my parents were proud I had become. I saw a chance to measure my success in miles rather than dollar signs. The happy future I had once imagined was long gone and I wasn't going to find solace in the purchase of a house or a reliable car to transport me back and forth from my couch to my desk.

Weeks turned into months as I thought of nothing but the trail. I obsessed over gear and mail drops and blogs. I slipped little details into conversation, trying to find something that hit home with my mom.

"Did you know that more than 3,000 people attempt to thru-hike the Appalachian Trail every year? So, I really never would be alone." and "There are tons of towns along the way to get supplies and I could call home every four or five days for most of the trip."

She grew more and more agitated every time I brought it up.

"I don't know why you're so set on this. Why you want to leave so badly," she snapped one day at lunch. We sat across from each other in a fake leather booth under a cheap mass-produced chandelier. She fixed her eyes on me, and they were unexpectedly venomous.

"I don't want to leave you! I'm just trying to live my life!" I snapped back.

"Live your life?!" Her voice was high and strained. "Christine, running away for six months in the woods is not *living your life*. Working this job and being there for your *dying* mother—that's living your life. I'm sorry it's not all glamour and adventure. But glamour and adventure aren't life." Her eyes swam.

"Stop being such a drama queen. You're not dying! I'm twenty-three years old. I need to live my life. I can't hang around here waiting for you to die. Why don't you just tell me when you're going to die, and I'll make sure to be there! Will it be next week? Next month? It could be ten years from now! Do you want me to stay here and hold your hand until then? You want me to put my life on hold and stay by your side until you die? That's ridiculous!"

How could my loving mother ever understand what I was truly running away from? Sure, it was easy for her to see me every day in my business casual, reporting to the overpaid position I had weaseled my way into. She wasn't there at three in the morning when I stumbled into bed, tripping over mountains of dirty laundry and passing out next to the latest stranger. It was easy for her to think I was running away from her. The truth was, I had already done that. Now, I was running away from the monster I had created in the process.

I needed to leave, but I couldn't tell her why. My life had become toxic. The only way to fix it was to leave it behind. I needed to be about something and there was nothing there for me to be about. On the Appalachian Trail I could be about hiking. It would replace all the other things I had been. I wouldn't have to ask myself who I was. I would be a hiker.

Preparing for a six-month hike can seem a bit daunting, even to an experienced backpacker, but to me it was a thrill a minute. Suddenly, I was a person who had something interesting to talk about; each new fact or facet learned was ammunition for the next conversation. I became single-minded, finding ways to bring up my plans in every conversation. I waited with bated breath until the appropriate moment arose, between "Hi, my name is" and "my degree is in business management", to provocatively announce "I'm preparing to thru-hike the Appalachian Trail!" The series of questions that inevitably followed this revelation was sheer delight.

"Where do you sleep?" *In or around shelters, they are all along the trail.*

"Where do you go to the bathroom?" *Almost every shelter has a privy, or you can dig a hole.*

"How do you shower?" *There are towns every five or six days. Yes, I plan to hike for five or six days without showering... gross, right?*

"What do you eat?" *Whatever is light and cheap and full of calories. I read a story about someone who ate nothing but Honey Buns the whole six months.*

"Are you going alone?"

"Are you going to carry a weapon?"

I never tired of discussing the logistics of bowel movements in the woods, my confidence with which was theoretical but unwavering, nonetheless. Of course, the more mundane topics always exhausted themselves quickly in comparison to the grander philosophical questions about being unmistakably female and existing alone for six months out in the untamed wilderness that is the Appalachian Trail.

To be fair, the AT is accessed by no fewer than two million

hikers annually, around 3,000 of which are attempting to thru-hike, so one could hardly claim to be "alone" at all. Try explaining that to your parents, coworkers, and friends as they present you with thoughtful gifts, like ten-inch survival knives complete with a six-foot length of paracord and a miniature magnifying glass (whatever that is used for). As my start date loomed, I was gifted several knives despite my assurances that I would not, in fact, be carrying a weapon. Unfortunately, nobody offered to buy me a warmer sleeping bag or a lighter tent.

Day 3: August 4, 2018

North Puyallup River → Devil's Dream

I STRETCH AND ROLL OVER, BURYING MY FACE INTO THE HOOD OF my sleeping bag against the chill. The light of the sun seeps through the walls of my tent by five a.m. this far north, so I have no idea what time it is. I think back on the conversation last night and wonder if Adam is awake yet or if he has already left.

"Christine." A loud stage whisper comes from right outside my tent.

I laugh out loud. "Good morning!" Running my fingers through my hair, I hurriedly escape my sleeping bag. "What time is it?" I pull on my day clothes and fumble with the zippers of the tent. From my position on the ground I gaze up at him.

"Just after seven," he says. He's wearing the same clothes as yesterday and chewing a bite of granola bar. Energy rolls off him in waves. "You ready to get going?"

"Maybe in ten minutes or so. You don't have to wait for me," I say.

"No worries, I can wait," he says with a grin. His bouncing

slows to a quivering vibration that could easily be mistaken for stillness.

Great, he can wait for me to get ready and then he can spend all day waiting for me to hike. Or he will see how sweaty I am and try to hide from me later. I didn't think we would hike together. Adam isn't just an ultra-light backpacker, he is compact—around 5'8" and no more than 140 pounds. At nearly 200 pounds with my pack on, I am no mountain goat.

Once my stove is going, I tear down my tent. Adam paces back and forth while I hastily pack up my things and scarf down two and a half servings of instant quinoa. That much food is going to weigh me down like a rock when I try to keep up with what will inevitably be a pace I struggle to match. Unfortunately, there isn't much practicality in saving leftovers for later when backpacking.

Having set a new personal record for time spent eating breakfast and breaking camp, I'm both ready and nervous to hit the trail. We stop on the bridge one last time to admire the power of the glacial river and share a collective sigh which would be audible if not for the crashing of the water.

Past the group site where my friends from yesterday are packing up, the trail starts to climb. We walk together for the first half-mile or so. I gasp and swallow inaudibly to avoid drawing attention to my eternal struggle. I regret the quinoa that sits heavily in my stomach.

Before long, Adam disappears around a switchback, allowing me to stop for a moment to catch my breath. It's easier to hike at my own pace when the faster person is out of sight, removing the pressure to keep up. I settle into my own rhythm and drag on a little further, still pushing myself harder than usual so I don't fall too far behind.

Around two miles into the uphill, I come around a corner to find the trail ahead opens to a spectacular view of Mt. Rainier. The network of glaciers encapsulating the summit is visible from this distance. Adam is standing at the next switchback gazing reverently at the mountain: the reason we are all here.

"Hey." I wipe my hot, rosy cheeks.

"Isn't this amazing?" Adam pulls out an old-school film camera.

"You're carrying a camera? In that tiny pack?" I demand.

"Yeah, the whole reason I am ultra-light is so I can carry this equipment," he says.

Adam takes several photos of the mountain then we each take one of the other, sweaty and exhausted. Those will look great, I'm sure. We start back up the hill and yo-yo the last mile to the Klapatche Park campsite—Adam pulling ahead and me catching up each time he stops to take pictures.

When I reach the campsite another group of hikers is preparing to leave. A small lake lies to the left of the trail; or perhaps it could more accurately be described as a mud hole after the week of record-breaking temperatures. The other group wastes no time in letting us know the lake makes a poor water source, but there is a better one about a mile ahead, prettier too.

My feet ache from the 1,750 ft climb and I want to soak them here and now. Filling my water reservoir can wait. Sitting on a log, I kick off my shoes and peel off my damp, sticky socks. The bandage on the bottom of my foot has melded with my big toe and shows no signs of loosening. I twinkle toes my bare feet across the trail until they press into the soft, dried mud which was once part of the lake bottom. As I sink into the cool water, hundreds of tadpoles scurry away—I hadn't noticed them before. Stooping to study them, I find each one has a small pair of legs sprouting from its little round body.

"Hey! The tadpoles are halfway to becoming frogs! They're so cute," I call over to Adam.

Adam stops taking photos to come investigate. His face lights up when he sees the tadpole-frogs. "They *are* so cute," he agrees.

We spend a good twenty minutes kicking around the swampy lake watching the tadpoles scatter as we approach and swarm around our feet in moments of stillness. Finally, we settle down near the water with snacks and congratulate each other on a well-spent morning.

A woman around my age appears down the trail from the same direction we came from and stops at the lake's edge past where we are sitting. She drops her monstrous pack and pulls out an apple—a bold choice considering the obvious weight-to-calorie inefficiency. Gazing into the lake, she munches with measured nonchalance. I know exactly how it feels to be alone and determinedly minding your own business around other groups of hikers.

I immediately decide we're going to be friends.

Jumping up from my seat, I stride the distance between us and squat down next to her.

"Hey, are you hiking alone?" I ask. It feels funny to ask this question rather than answer it. I make sure not to come off as accusatory or concerned. We're on the same side.

"Yeah," she replies.

"Me too! And so is Adam." I wave Adam over to join us. "We met last night, but we're headed to the same place today."

"Oh, cool, I'm Jenna." We shake hands like old pals.

"Christine. Where are you headed tonight?" I ask.

"Devil's Dream," she says, without even pulling a sour face. She must not know.

"Us too! We can all be friends, three friends hiking alone together. We have heard the bugs are horrible there, so we're planning to stop at Indian Henry's for dinner and hang out for a while and then head into Devil's Dream in time for bed," I ramble on enthusiastically.

"Sounds great, where else are you guys camping? I got a walk-up permit for six days, and a bunch of my campsites are off trail since they were the only ones left." Jenna frowns.

"I got a walk up-permit too, but I'm hiking for twelve days, so I'm camping just about everywhere. Adam is hiking in six days too, but he got all the good spots in the lottery. You should mooch onto his campsites and stay at the good places. You guys can be best friends," I suggest like an asinine know-it-all.

She looks eagerly over at Adam. "Could I? Is that allowed?"

He agrees, and my heart sinks. They're going to run off and be best friends. I only approached her because I thought she might be my new best friend and now I've messed it all up.

We share our stories about how backpacking has changed our lives and how we got into it. We have vastly different histories, but they all feel relatable. We jump right into the intimate details, skipping the small talk completely.

"I wish real life was like this. You meet cool people at random and talk about real shit," Adam says exactly what I was thinking. One of the main reasons I enjoy backpacking alone is the community. When you are open to it and not shielding yourself from outside interaction, it can be such beautiful company.

Jenna announces it's time to get hiking again and we heckle her for not putting her feet in the lake. She surrenders and takes off her shoes, but her heart isn't in it and she's back on the trail shortly thereafter.

Only three miles into an almost fifteen-mile day, I push worry out of my head. If not for Adam, I would never take a full break so early in the day. I've always been such a slow hiker that an hour-long break before noon seems preposterous, even though I know the miles can easily be completed in six or seven hours. Watching Jenna attack her day with a sense of urgency reminds me to slow down and enjoy every moment. Appreciating this spot is just as important as making the day's miles.

Eventually we move along, knowing St. Andrew's Lake is a mile away and we will have to stop to collect water at the very least. The next mile is equally as steep as the previous three before we finally reach the lake. Jenna crouches on the nearest bank collecting water, but Adam suggests we circle the lake and I reluctantly agree. Adding steps to my longest day wasn't what I had in mind. When we arrive at the opposite side of the lake, Jenna is already heading back on the trail. We collect water and Adam immediately goes back into break mode. He's wading out into St. Andrew's Lake wearing his full pack and carrying his camera.

"Get in!" he calls to me.

We just took a break. I need to hike. I don't want to take my shoes off again. I don't want to put them back on again.

"I'm good!" I don't want to look like a stick in the mud, but I should probably take off and let him catch up. He is charming and carefree, walking around in the lake, marveling aloud at the beauty of Mt. Rainier looming above us and the pristine alpine lake.

"If you had to choose between oceans, rivers, and alpine lakes, which would you choose?" he asks from the middle of the lake, up to his thighs in the water. His tiny running shorts are dangerously close to getting soaked.

"I love the ocean," I reply, "there is nothing like floating behind the first break, rising and falling with the rhythm of the waves."

I've never understood the quintessential outdoors question: ocean or mountains? I have always felt a kinship with the ocean, and the mountains are a relatively new player in my life. There is no comparison, they are apples and oranges, both amazing in their own right. As I consider his question, I continue, "But I love an alpine lake. Some of my favorite hiking memories are of plunging into a freezing lake of snowmelt and jumping right back out again to dry in the sun."

"You can't beat this!" He gestures grandly and I can't argue with him. I may love the ocean, but how can you be present in such a beautiful place and not love it more than anything else? It is real and encompassing, and is there any greater love than presence? I think of my mom's confusion at my desire to backpack. Her baffled face when I described the Appalachian Trail to her the first time. And the hundredth. I wonder how anyone could know that places like this exist and be completely disinterested in being here. The draw of the mountains pulls at my heart. In Adam's pure joy, I see a heart like mine.

———

The trail descends from the lake and, though we left together only minutes ago, I find myself walking alone. Being left behind again has me filled with angst and uncertainty. The feeling of being punched in the stomach is one I am familiar with. My body isn't made for speed. Every time I fall behind, feelings of inadequacy flood me and tears threaten.

Since my time on the Appalachian Trail I have worked to build a relationship with my body—learning to love and trust it. It's been a complicated journey, but I've found the best way to appreciate my body is to avoid comparing it to others, and the easiest way to avoid comparison is to hike alone. I have gotten stronger and faster than I ever thought I could be, and when I backpack alone I appreciate how far I've come. As soon as I attempt to keep pace with others it becomes obvious that I'm more deserving of the "Most Improved" award, the kind I used to scoff at in school. Maybe my best performance will never compete with my peers.

A deep cleansing breath reminds me of my intention to hike slow and spend time alone. The purpose of this trip was to help me clear my head and reset from my time in Portland. I spent the last two months trying desperately to manifest a romantic connection in a city that didn't make me feel full. Now I've escaped to a beautiful mountain overflowing with love and joy and I allow myself to be distracted by a boy—a boy from the same city I was so relieved to have just left.

My sigh is as heavy and loud as my footsteps. Today is the longest day of my itinerary, and there are two more big uphill climbs ahead of me. A 1,500 ft ascent is followed shortly by another 1,000 ft—a challenge that at one time would have been not only daunting, but unfathomable, is now a manageable pursuit. When I reach the South Puyallup River campground, I convince myself to stop for fuel, even though I'm not on empty yet.

Jenna is posted up in one of the campsites with the contents of her pack spread around. I settle in next to her for an intense discussion on the merits of different clothing layering options. She immediately convinces me I need to trade out my tank top and wool long sleeve for a synthetic long sleeve, which can be worn in all weather. Talking gear is a quintessential component of a thru-hike, and I've always been fascinated by the myriad of ways people do essentially the same activity.

Jenna offers me some weed which I decline. She leans against her massive pack smoking—she's cool, relaxed. She's taken down her wavy hair and it's impossibly long and shiny. After a season on the Pacific Crest Trail, her angular face is a deep bronze, and her muscles are lean and strong. She's in her element on the trail—she fits here like the log we sit on and the streams we cross. I imagined myself becoming this way once, but it never came to pass. I remain soft, frizzy, uncool.

———

We set off together, but Jenna quickly pulls ahead, leaving me to plod along behind. I drag myself up Emerald Ridge, a surprisingly steep and challenging ascent. For at least half an hour I think the climb must end any second, but it doesn't relent. My quadriceps burn with every step, pushing the weight of my body and my pack ever so slowly uphill. At last, I reach flatter ground and the top of the ridge is revealed.

There isn't another human in sight. "Wow," I gasp and pant.

A grassy meadow is splayed out to the right. Two marmots frolic through pink and orange wildflowers. Marmots always seem to be displaying their boisterous personalities. When they aren't moving, they're posing, making themselves the perfect subject for an alpine photo shoot. When I stop to take a photo, I realize my phone battery has already drained.

Oh well, nine days without having to look at my phone.

My goofy grin persists as I start down the other side of Emerald Ridge. I made it up that crazy hill! There are millions of people who will never see this. Quitting my job and spending my days on the trail were the best decisions ever. I never want to leave. Maybe I should just live here. I don't need anyone else; I have this mountain and these marmots. What more could a girl ask for?

As I skip down the other side of the ridge, I cross paths with a couple hiking the other direction. They are huffing and puffing and leaning hard into their trekking poles—the descent is actually quite steep. We exchange hellos. They ask how far, and I assure them the top of the ridge is near and the views are beyond spectacular. They smile ardently to each other and continue up with renewed vigor. I feel a pang of envy at their connection.

My thoughts swing wildly back and forth, giving me emotional whiplash as the next few miles disappear beneath my feet. When the trail shifts upward once again, I know I've reached the last mile and a half before Indian Henry's. I consider stopping for water at one of the stream crossings near the low point, but the last few miles have been so leisurely that I don't much feel like taking a break. I'm keen to meet back up with Adam and Jenna at Indian Henry's, and a mile and a half rarely takes more than thirty minutes—even if it's uphill.

Objectively speaking, this ascent is no more challenging than the last one, by now my legs are trembling. Each step feels like a momentous effort, and the emotional exhaustion of the day is weighing me down. I remember thinking about turning back on the first day and consider that if I had gone back to the city and saved myself the hassle of climbing up and down and up and down all these peaks and valleys, I wouldn't be here, in this moment. The light that only comes from connecting deeply with this crazy planet crowds out the soreness, fatigue, and doubt about whether I even like backpacking.

Sweat soaks my shirt and drips from my chin. I steadily sip water as I climb, grateful for the genius invention of the water bladder. Suddenly, I feel the telltale pressure change in my mouthpiece signaling the water has run out. Water bladders have no water level indicator. Indian Henry's must be close, so even if there isn't another stream before it, I can always borrow some water from one of my cohorts when I get there. There have been plentiful and regular water sources in the last three days, and there's no reason to think there won't be one around the next corner.

I quickly start to deteriorate. My mouth turns dry and cottony, and it seems like I'm sweating more than ever. All my precious water is leaking out of me. I suck at the mouthpiece, hoping for another sip. The umbles come on quickly—I'm stumbling and bumbling. My feet are clumsy beneath me. Has it been five minutes or twenty-five minutes since I ran out of water? It's hard to say. My eyelids grow heavy—I bend over with my hands on my knees to take a few steadying breaths. I know the most dangerous thing to do in the woods is allow myself to become disoriented. I *must* be nearly there.

On repeat I whisper, "Keep walking. Don't panic. Stay on the trail."

I stop and sit on a rock to clear my head. Yanking my hydration bladder from my pack, I turn it upside down and drink the last half ounce below the hose. This feels like true desperation and I need to keep a level head. Adam and Jenna are expecting me and have probably been waiting for hours already. They hike so fast, and I'm taking a stupid long time to walk this last mile and a half. I imagine their conversation.

Where is Christine? I hope she's okay. Oh, she's probably fine, she is just SO slow. I can't even believe she hikes, seems like she'd give it up. Is it even fun when you're that slow? Seems kind of miserable.

As soon as I start back up the trail, I think I can hear water trickling. Is it an auditory mirage—a figment of my parched imagination? I've never become delirious from dehydration on the trail and have no idea what my mind is capable of. Staring at my feet, I will them to take one step and then another. The sound of water seems to grow louder. Another grueling hundred yards pass before I arrive at the edge of a tiny mountain stream burbling happily across the trail. I fling my pack in the middle of the trail and pull out my filter and water bottle. I filter twenty ounces of water in my first bag and greedily drink it all. The water is cold and tastes pristine. Municipal water will never compare to a filtered mountain stream.

I think of my parents and their concern for my safety. When imagining me meeting my demise in the wilderness, perhaps they had envisioned a bear devouring my entrails or a man lunging from the shadows to bind my wrists and drag me into the depths of the forest. I don't know that they gave much thought to more mundane dangers. Those of poor planning or overexertion. Dehydration isn't a particularly glamorous way to die.

Adam and Jenna are probably wondering where I am, so I fill my water bladder and get back on the trail right away. While it would be better to take a few minutes to let my system absorb and recover, I push on. It's a pleasant surprise that Indian Henry's is only ten minutes away. When

I emerge from the trees and see them sitting on the porch of a picturesque log cabin, I yell, "Wow!" and they both look up and wave.

"This is beautiful!" Adam calls across the meadow. They both nod vigorously.

"How long have you guys been here?" I must know.

"Like fifteen/twenty minutes?" Jenna looks to Adam for confirmation. He agrees.

Maybe I'm not that slow after all. Was I making good time while thinking I was going to die? Or maybe they took a ton of breaks. Were they hiking together this whole time? Are they best friends now?

"Oh, that's not so bad! You guys ready for dinner?" I ask, as if the last half mile hadn't had me nearly on my knees.

We sit in a circle on the porch, surrounded by our things, surrounded by nature. I boil water for my dinner: oatmeal with almond butter and freeze-dried strawberries and bananas. Jenna prepares a hot dinner and Adam eats another granola bar. I offer him hot tea—I've found his weakness. He may pretend to enjoy cold oatmeal but having nothing warm for six days in a row must be demoralizing.

"What do you guys think about staying here for the night?" Surprisingly, the suggestion is Jenna's and not mine. The meadow is sprawled out like a lawn in front of the cabin. The trail crosses a stream twice as it cuts through the grass and flowers, and trees frame the whole scene.

"I mean, we could either stay here." I gesture around at the paradise before us. "Or we could hike another mile to the 'worst campsite on the trail' and be eaten alive by mosquitoes all night."

"Do you think we'll get in trouble if we stay here?" Jenna seems uncertain. In most situations I wouldn't condone unapologetic rule breaking either.

"I'm pretty tired, and when I got my permit, they *did* say not to risk my safety to make my reservations. I would feel a lot safer camping here, instead of pushing myself any further today. I don't think they'd give us a hard time if we stay," I propose with a wink.

We share a conspiratorial look, and it's decided—we'll stay. As the sun sinks lower in the sky the mosquitoes materialize, and we commiserate that at least they can't be as bad as Devil's Dream. Jenna and I start unpacking our tents.

"You're going to set up tents? When we have this great porch to sleep on?" Adam frowns.

"Oh, I'm setting up my tent ON the porch," Jenna assures him.

"I think I'll be right in front of the steps here on the dirt. My tent isn't freestanding, and I don't want to disturb the meadow," I explain my plan.

My offer from the night before hangs in the air between me and Adam. I want him to share my tent, to lay beside me. I wonder if he won't because we aren't staying in Devil's Dream. Or because she's here. Or because I'm too slow. Or too sweaty.

"You're going to let me get eaten by mosquitoes alone?" he groans.

It seems like the question is directed at Jenna, and I wonder if my eyes are literally green with envy.

"I already told you, you can sleep in my tent." I try to sound playful and casual but imagine it sounds something more like pathetically desperate.

He likes her, they have way more in common than we do. He's just not that into me.

I look away from them and continue setting up my tent. I

should have just died of dehydration back there and avoided this embarrassment.

There is a painfully long silence, and then, "Oh yeah, okay."

———

Jenna announces she is going to bed, so Adam and I retire to my tent. He asks if we can leave the rainfly off so he can watch the stars. I never sleep without the rainfly when I'm alone, but it feels safe with him. It's the little details like this which make it difficult to pretend being a woman alone doesn't shape my experiences. We settle into our sleeping bags and I agonize over what is the right amount of physical contact. I timidly wrap my arm around Adam's waist, he says nothing.

My Alps Mountaineering Mystique 1.5 tent is an unusual size intended for one and a half persons. The space is ideal for a girl and her gear, or a girl and her dog, but not quite right for a girl and her boy. The tent is widest at the shoulders, where two sleeping pads can comfortably fit side by side. The area toward the bottom is considerably narrower, creating an overlap of pads and a mashup of sleeping bag foot boxes and feet.

I snuggle into Adam's warmth and find that I am awash with a confusion of emotions. My loneliness strikes again. Our palpable lack of enthusiasm for the situation is uncomfortably mutual. I had thought that lying in his arms would bring comfort, or a sense of companionship.

Battling my insecurity in real time, I ask if I can put my hand under his shirt. I want to be closer. He agrees and I find the bottom of his shirt, sliding my hand over his firm stomach and up to feel the surprising amount of hair on his chest. There is no romantic connection here, only the comfort of skin-to-skin contact. I melt into him, his arm around me and my head resting on his chest.

My fingers trace slow circles and swirls on his skin, measuring his reaction, but he is motionless—his breathing steady. He is unfazed. I have spent years throwing myself at beautiful men trying to prove my worth; each notch on my bedpost a tragic attempt at propping up my fragile self-esteem. His ambivalence is physically painful to me—I obsess over what he's thinking about, and what he thinks about me.

Nervous energy keeps me awake for nearly an hour. Adam unzips the tent periodically to look out at the stars without that pesky mesh obstructing his view.

Chapter 4

As part of my preparation for the Appalachian Trail, I moved to Yosemite National Park in August 2014. I planned to stay until January working as a cashier in the gift shop. This would give me enough time to hike and camp to practice for 2,000 miles of backpacking. It would also be an opportunity to hang out with real rugged outdoors people, to observe them in their natural habitat and learn their ways. Then I planned to spend two months back at my parents' house in Arkansas figuring out logistics and packing for the trail before my anticipated start date in mid-March.

My aspirations of physical conditioning and practice backpacking could easily be described as ambitious. My execution of them—nearly nonexistent. Yosemite in August is brutally hot and dry, and the elevation in the valley is almost 4,000 ft. The hiking trails ascending to its granite heights are steep paths that zigzag aggressively up sunbaked slabs of rock. I had no idea what I was getting into.

My first week of work, I made a friend in employee orientation. Jeff thought I was cute; I could tell right away, but I wasn't sure about him. He was blonde and tan, with a surfer's drawl and a southern California attitude. Everything was chill to Jeff. At the end of training, he asked if I wanted to go for a hike.

Of course I did, that's what I came to Yosemite for.

When we met for our hike, I let him lead the way. Jeff's stride was quick and confident, unlike his voice and demeanor. My t-shirt clung to my sweaty body before we were out of sight of the Happy Isles trailhead. As I struggled to keep up with his aggressive pace, I knew this was doomed to be a repeat of my tearful day of hiking with Taylor. I should never have agreed to this.

Coming from Arkansas, I had yet to acclimate to the increase in elevation. The inside of my nose cracked and bled from the lack of humidity and there wasn't enough water in California during a record-breaking drought to stay hydrated. Following behind Jeff, I leaned heavily into my trekking poles and pushed myself forward through the dusty heat. Each time he realized how far behind I had fallen he would stop and wait for me to catch up, only to turn on his heel and continue ahead as soon as I arrived.

If you want to make a slow person cry on a hike, this is a great tactic.

The first mile of the Mist Trail gains about 300 feet. Most hikers would describe this type of ascent as gentle or, dare I say it, flat. But with the heat of the day and Jeff's judgmental glances over his shoulder, I might as well have been on a staircase to the sun. When we finally reached the footbridge beneath Vernal Falls, from which a view of the measly cascade was possible, I was done.

Jeff smiled hopefully as I slumped against the wooden railing. If he couldn't sense my defeat, he must have been willfully ignorant. I gazed into the trickle of water, wondering if I was only fooling myself. I'd told so many people about my plans for the Appalachian Trail—I couldn't go back on them now. I would have to hike 2,000 miles whether I liked it or not. And if this one mile was any indication, I wasn't going to like it.

Jeff's attempts to cajole me to the top of Vernal Falls were half-hearted and not well-received. I could see that the trail beyond the bridge quickly morphed into a treacherously uneven stone staircase that wrapped along the edge of the falls. There was no way I would go any further that day. Maybe next time. Jeff didn't hide his disappointment at the shortness of the hike or his laughter at my ambitions of hiking the Appalachian Trail. He probably didn't think I was cute anymore. I definitely didn't think he was.

———

Aside from hiking, I had come to Yosemite to be part of an outdoors community. In my previous life, I didn't know many people who hiked, so I had learned everything up until that point from the internet. I hoped my hike with Jeff wasn't indicative of my chances of fitting in to the community here. When I looked around employee housing, I expected to see hundreds of fit, tan super-hikers walking around with fifty-liter packs on their backs. What I found was a combination of dirty rock climbers, burnout college kids, and seemingly ordinary people.

My first week after employee orientation, I met the badass hiker woman I had been searching for, but I didn't recognize her for what she was. Laura was tan and very thin, all elbows and hairy legs. Her sun-bleached hair hung un-styled around her angular face and big plastic frame glasses. She wore a long skirt and a cardigan—she could have worked at a store anywhere. She was ordinary and she was teaching me how to ring up bananas.

When I mentioned my plans to hike the Appalachian Trail, Laura's eyebrows shot up.

"That's great, I'd love to do something like that! Where have you backpacked before?" she asked.

"I haven't really, I'm hoping to practice while I'm here," I said.

"Oh! This is a great place to practice." She nodded her head enthusiastically.

Her encouragement was welcome after my embarrassing hike with Jeff.

The next week, she told me she had hiked Mt. Whitney on her weekend.

"What's Mt. Whitney?" I asked.

"The tallest mountain in the Continental US," she said.

"Was it hard?" I wanted to know.

"Not really, it's just long. Twenty-two miles," she said.

"Were there any really steep parts?" I asked.

"No, just a ton of switchbacks."

"How long did it take you?"

"About nine hours," she answered.

"Maybe I could do that," I paused, thinking, "I can walk for a long time if it's not insanely steep."

"Oh yeah, you should totally do it!" Her face lit up.

She looked at me and saw somebody that could do what she had done. I failed to recognize our misunderstanding.

———

The next week, I stood atop Mt. Whitney. Against all odds and at great risk to my health and safety, I had slogged the eleven miles to 14,500 feet. It was reckless at best, but it had to be done. The rocky summit was deserted when I arrived. I had been walking for sixteen hours, and it was past five p.m.—nobody in their right minds would be up here this late.

High altitude mountains demand an early summit, as deadly storms can arise almost instantaneously in the afternoons. I didn't know the danger, even as I peered inside the stone lightning shelter that marked the peak. Gusty winds whipped at my bare legs and I wrapped my arms tightly around myself. The bright light of the sun forced my eyes nearly shut and I wondered if I should feel elated—all I could muster was tearful exhaustion.

Jeff's voice rang in my ears. "You'll never make it to the top of Mt Whitney; you couldn't even hike the Mist Trail."

He was right about the past, but not about the future. I summited Mt Whitney on my own terms. I didn't try to match pace with someone much faster than me, I didn't wear myself out mentally thinking about how inadequate I was. And I wasn't going to let that guy tell me what I could or couldn't do. The past doesn't always know the future. When we decide it's time to grow and change, it's not our past that tells us how. We look ahead at who we want to be and seek out a path to get there.

I wanted to be a woman who hiked the Appalachian Trail. That woman could keep hiking when her legs were tired, the air was thin, and her skin was burned. So that's what I did. Because the woman I wanted to be couldn't exist until I did those things. She was counting on me to get there.

I cursed spitefully at the sign at the trailhead. At one o'clock that morning, I had read the warning. "REMEMBER: The top is only half-way." But now, the prospect of walking another eleven miles seemed unfathomable. Impossible. Absurd.

My feet directed themselves back to the trail of their own

accord. The signals from legs to brain were crisscrossed and faint. The pain and tightness of my calf and quad muscles had become numb somewhere along the way. I stumbled down for hours into darkness, tripping over my boots. Stars twinkled to life above me. The glowing eyes of deer appeared often in the narrow beam of my headlamp. Each time, my pulse quickened but my legs continued forward at the same trudging pace. What if something more threatening than a deer had appeared in my narrow shaft of visibility? I had nothing left to give. No survival instinct remained. Only walking zombie-like through the night.

———

It took more than a week to recover physically from Mt Whitney. The ill-conceived trip left me broken, dehydrated, and nearly unable to walk. I announced proudly to all that would hear that I had hiked Mt Whitney. Laura was impressed, but I was even more impressed with her—now that I understood what she had done. She was a super-hiker and I wanted her to be my friend.

Most of my coworkers congratulated me. One woman asked me how long it took. When I told her twenty-four hours, she laughed in my face.

"It took you twenty-four HOURS to hike Mt Whitney?" she shouted gleefully.

"How long did it take you?" I asked, my face red with shame—and sunburn.

"I haven't hiked Mt Whitney," she said.

I had forced myself excruciatingly up that mountain and back down. I had fallen to my knees in the parking lot. I had proven that I could keep going when my body and my mind were telling me to quit. Yet, I was still not good enough for this woman. Luckily, this woman wasn't the woman I wanted to become.

The next week, Laura and I made plans to drive up to Glacier Point for sunrise. There was a massive fire burning just behind Half Dome, filling the valley with smoke and scaring away visitors. We wanted to see it for ourselves. We invited another employee who'd arrived around the same time I did. Lindy and I had been assigned neighboring tent homes and made fast friends.

The three of us rose before four o'clock and piled into Laura's car. As she took the windy turns up to the top of Glacier Point Road, we rubbed the sleep from our eyes. The first light of dawn hadn't yet begun to peek out from behind the granite walls and the still silence seemed to swallow up the sounds of our shuffling feet and stifled yawns. We sat on the edge of the stone wall, overlooking our little kingdom. From 3,000 feet above, we could see only pinpricks of light shining up from the valley floor.

The sun finally began to rise, a dim crimson orb buried behind layers of cloud and smoke. The light was diffuse and strange. It was almost impossible to see an end to the smoke from our vantage. I looked down into the valley again, realizing just how small our little speck of civilization was. The hungry flames consumed everything in their path and could devour us and our homes in an instant.

"I just learned that the giant sequoias can only reproduce with fire," Lindy said in a hushed voice. "It may seem like the fire is destructive, but it's actually the key to life. The pinecones are so tightly bound that the seeds won't be released without extreme heat. Plus, it clears away the dead stuff and makes room for new growth. The fire is part of the life cycle of the valley."

I looked over at my two new friends. We'd known each

other only a couple weeks, but their friendship already meant more to me than a sunrise drive and a new perspective. They were the fresh start I was looking for. They represented the things I wanted to be—active and thoughtful. Full of joy and connection.

I had thought I was burning my old life down to make room for my own growth. I wanted to become bigger and take up more space. But it seemed that enough room had cleared for new relationships too.

———

As the heat of summer dissipated, the appeal of hiking went with it. I settled into a routine in Yosemite Valley, working closing shifts at the Village Store and hanging out with Lindy and Laura. We became friends. Real friends. Not the kind of friends who meet you at the bar on a Tuesday night to drink away the day—the kind who drink steaming cups of tea by the fireplace and walk to work together.

Lindy and I became inseparable. We worked the same shifts, stood across the register bay from each other, laughed at customers after they left. We competed fiercely for the weekly free sandwich to the cashier who sold the most reusable bags. We yelled to each other across the ten feet of empty space between the vinyl wall of my tent platform and hers.

We were the same in some ways, but so different in others. Before work every day, Lindy showered, styled her hair, and put on makeup. Her routines baffled me—most of the employees in the park seemed to be competing in an unspoken game of *Who Can Go the Longest Between Showers*, and I figured it was good practice for the trail. She sometimes lovingly told me she could smell me from across the room (a sure sign that I was winning the game). She offered to comb my unruly hair, which hadn't been cut since before my mom's diagnosis and hung past the middle of my back.

I would sit before her on my knees while she gently brushed out my tangles. She marveled at the thick wavy mass of my hair, so different than her tight shoulder length curls. She wanted to know why I refused to brush my hair. I couldn't quite explain it—I wanted it to care for itself.

I didn't know about her mother, who struggled with depression and sometimes went weeks without washing or brushing her hair. We tried to explain who we were and how we had come to be in this place, always delicately tiptoeing around the subject of the women we had been asked to be. We were both silently rebelling against the idea of becoming our mothers—both trying to figure out what that meant to us.

———

Before winter set in, we assembled a group for an overnight backpacking trip. The group was evenly split between experienced backpackers and others like me. Lindy was in the latter category. We were eager though, and that counts for something.

When we set off from the trailhead, we were a group of seven. The rest of the group quickly pulled away and Lindy and I became a group of two. We huffed and puffed as if we had some hope of keeping up, but we were hopeless. Hunched beneath the weight of our packs, we dragged our feet along the trail. There was nothing good to say and not enough oxygen to complain, so we allowed the stomping of our stiff heavy boots to fill the air.

"You don't have to wait for me," Lindy offered as we stopped to catch our breath for the hundredth time.

A generous thought, as if I could have gone any faster.

She must have thought I could, I was going to hike the Appalachian Trail after all. I wondered again if I had fooled myself into thinking I could hike two thousand plus miles.

We finally accepted that the rest of the group was long gone and settled into our own rhythm. I watched as Lindy stopped to take photos, to wonder after beautiful plants and interesting stones. Each time, I thought we ought to be pushing harder. I wondered what the rest of the group must have been thinking of us for being so slow. Lindy was unconcerned. At her snail's pace, she seemed to truly be enjoying herself. I didn't understand how it was possible. We were hardly moving and *still* struggling. Everyone would laugh at us.

I thought again of my hikes with Taylor and Jeff. Of my overwhelming shame, the anger I've directed at my body for being such a disappointment. But the beaming grin on Lindy's face conveyed nothing of shame and disappointment. She was filled with pride under her overstuffed borrowed backpack. Speed wasn't something she expected of her body. She moved at a pace that felt comfortable to her.

"You really don't have to wait," Lindy said again, "I don't mind hiking alone."

Perhaps I could have hiked a bit faster, but not by much. We could have spent the day slowly inching apart as I pushed myself onward with the sheer force of self-loathing while she moseyed along behind. I never would have kept up with the others. But instead, we spent the day getting closer—bonding over the shared challenge and our obvious ineptitude.

When we finally reached camp, exhaustion overwhelmed me. The tents were erected and sleeping bags laid out in rows. The piercing cold was unbearable at 11,000 feet, so I huddled in the tent while everyone else stood out under the stars drinking from flasks of whiskey and premixed margaritas. Laughter echoed through the night as if I had been dropped into a canyon full of hyenas. I laid in the near pitch darkness, eyes peeled wide, staring up against the nylon roof of the girls' tent.

My first attempt at backpacking wasn't going at all how I had imagined. There were five people more physically capable than I was and I wondered if I had what it took to hike the Appalachian Trail after all. Hiking never seemed to get any easier. My legs never seemed to get any stronger. Seeing Lindy was what truly opened my eyes. She was someone who was about something. Not hiking. Joy.

———

In the seventeen months between discovering the Appalachian Trail and stepping foot at the Southern Terminus on top of Springer Mountain in north Georgia, I had left my old self behind. Leaving my job and leaving my parents in Arkansas was easy. It felt necessary in many ways—a step toward who I wanted to become. Leaving my new friends in Yosemite was much harder. The valley and the people in it had breathed new life into me. Even with the plans I had made and all the work I had done to get there, it was difficult to head east again from California. In January, I drove the 1,800 miles back to Arkansas alone.

Day 4: August 5, 2018
Indian Henry's → Pyramid Creek

ADAM DRAGS HIS BEDDING OUT OF MY TENT BEFORE I OPEN MY EYES. He and Jenna have another long day ahead of them, so they pack up early. Cutting my day short by one mile yesterday means I will be hiking three miles instead of two on my shortest scheduled day—a fair trade-off. The sun shines as if today is any other day, but I feel exposed under its light. I'm ashamed of my need for constant affirmation. I didn't come out here to meet some guy, and somehow the appearance of some guy immediately made me forget my purpose.

Hiding out in my tent for the foreseeable future sounds appealing—though it would be wise to dispose of the evidence of our illegal campsite. I pack up my things, and we eat breakfast on the porch. Adam and Jenna say a totally casual goodbye and head down the trail. Adam looks back as he walks away—we nod, some small closure after an uncomfortable evening. A silent pact to forget this ever happened.

With no reason to rush the day, I putter around the cabin and allow them to put some space between us. A meditative peace comes over me as I watch the microscopic wave of the grasses and flowers in the meadow and listen to the sounds of nothing. Light breezes come and go as I sit with myself for the better part of an hour. Being alone again brings an equanimity—the pressure to connect assuaged as soon as the prospect is removed. The commitment to making a meaningful connection each day suddenly feels clunky and unnecessary.

Across the meadow, a group of trail runners appear from the shadow of the forest. They're dressed in brightly colored shorts and tank tops with compression arm and calf sleeves. Running vests and hats complete loud sporty ensembles. Once upon a time, I would have been bitter about these people running by on a trail I was struggling to walk, now I revere them. Just as I once viewed the thru-hiking community as something I wanted to be part of, I now look longingly at the trail runners.

The runners pause to take photos of Indian Henry's cabin. Their voices carry across the meadow. I can't make out the words, but the camaraderie and joy are obvious even from a distance. It's still early, so they must have started in Longmire this morning, already covering six miles while I haven't even left camp. As they move along, I remind myself that backpacking is exciting and physically challenging. The comparison trap is easily laid because in the world of mountains, there will always be someone doing something bigger, better, and crazier.

I can't yet bring myself to leave such a beautiful place with only three miles to travel and no idea how the next campsite will compare. A while later, a woman emerges from the trees in front of the cabin traveling clockwise. She introduces herself as she drops her pack with a thud and sags onto the porch. When I ask if she is hiking alone, she shares that she left her group for the day because they were annoying her. Apparently, the other woman she was hiking with accidentally took a sleeping pill instead of her thyroid medication, and not for the first time. This is hilarious, as an outsider, but I don't know that I would have patience for such a mistake either.

Speaking to the woman reminds me that while there is warmth in companionship on the trail, there are also challenges. When she leaves, I spend some time reflecting on my situation. I want to be able to do things like this alone because I know I can't count on anyone else. I want to be able to dream my own dreams and not wait around for a partner. I never want to have to live up to someone else's expectations or expect anything from someone else.

———

Around noon, I do some standing stretches and eat a granola bar before hitting the trail. The one-mile stretch to Devil's Dream passes quickly. Admittedly, we could have easily made it there last night if we'd wanted to. In checking out the area, I'm glad we didn't forfeit the scenery at Indian Henry's for these monochromatic brown surroundings. The site is nestled among the trunks of tall trees. It's cool and shady in the noon sun. There are no noteworthy features except the buzzing flies and mosquitoes.

With no reason to linger, I keep moving and arrive at Pyramid Creek camp within the hour. I immediately regret leaving Indian Henry's, as this campsite has little more to offer than Devil's Dream. The dive-bombing flies and mosquitoes are annoying while hiking, and unbearable when I stop moving. They buzz and tap and bite, drawing on my blood and my patience.

I notice the wear on my pack as I drop it to the ground. The spongy undersides of the straps are a dingy brown with the sweat they've absorbed during my cumulative time on trails. As I set up my little tent, I run my fingers over the small tear beside the zipper and the runs in the mesh. I've stared up at this ceiling for countless nights. Through these walls, I've listened to the buzzing of mosquitoes, the howling of the wind, and the footsteps of my fellow adventurers. I unfurl my sleeping bag and make my bed, moving my belongings here and there, like I always do. Lastly, I pick up my trekking poles and study them for a moment. The metal tip of one is bent at a slight angle and the basket has long been missing from the other. The cork handles are scratched and filthy— they would likely make a fascinating subject for bacterial analysis. These are the poles that held my hands along the Appalachian Trail, and many times since.

These worn out items are practically worthless. Honestly, I probably couldn't even give them away. But when I hold each one, their value is immeasurable. They are more than the tools that have facilitated my journey. They are the friends that have accompanied me along the way. They've each been an integral part of the miles I've walked and a testament to the work I've put in. Hiking has never gotten much easier, but I've sure done a lot of it, and I don't plan to quit any time soon.

––––––––

It must be at least four in the afternoon and still nobody else has arrived. Purely for something to do, I go to retrieve my food bag. The bear pole must be fifteen feet high—the rod with which I raise and lower my bag of food is hardly long enough to reach and unwieldy besides. I stagger beneath the weight of my food at the end of a ten-foot pole, before losing control and bringing it to the ground with a crash.

I am confounded, trying to imagine how a shorter person would even hang their food. The Wonderland Trail was established in 1915, but I would guess the bear poles were put up significantly later. Apparently, when this one was erected, it was assumed all hikers were 5'10" or taller. They must not have been planning for many women.

I heat up water for my dinner oatmeal, stir in some wild blueberries and sit at the bottom of the bear pole eating from a collapsible silicone cup. As I rinse my cup and prepare to rehang my food, a couple comes in the main entrance of the camp.

They stop in the first campsite, visible from my perch, and the woman unceremoniously drops her oversized pack. The guy heads up the main path toward me and we exchange greetings. He asks about the other sites. I assure him they are all about equal as far as space and view goes; big, flat, and brown.

"I'm Noah, and that's Sara."

"I'm Christine, can I come hang out with you guys for a little bit? I've been alone here for hours!"

"Totally, we are pretty tired of each other by now." Noah laughs.

I smile, even though I don't find the joke particularly funny.

"We usually do dinner around six if you want to come over," he says.

"Sure, what time is it now?" I ask. Now that my phone is dead, I don't have any way to tell time.

"Just before 5," he says as he turns back down the trail.

I spend the next hour washing my dirty clothing. It's so warm and dry here in August that they dry almost instantly.

Around six o'clock, I find Sara and Noah boiling water for their nine-dollar pre-packaged freeze-dried dinners. I note the difference between food on the Wonderland Trail and the Appalachian Trail. On the AT, cheap food creativity is the name of the game, but here the freeze-dried gourmet feels ubiquitous. I had grown accustomed to witnessing abominable concoctions such as ramen, thickened with powdered mashed potatoes, topped with pepperoni slices and peanut butter, and wrapped in a tortilla. The civility of eating a bag of Pad Thai now seems almost absurd.

We discuss and compare the merits of carrying a one- or two-person tent. Unlike Adam, these two seem to be carrying medium-weight everything AND fifteen pounds of camera equipment. I marvel at the idea of backpacking with a partner and not sharing any gear weight.

Noah mentions that he hiked the Appalachian Trail a few years previous.

"I did the AT in 2015!" I say. "Well... a big chunk of it." The qualification sticks a bit in my throat.

"Oh yeah? How much?" he demands.

"650 miles." I shrug.

"About a quarter of the trail." He quickly does the math.

Hmm! More like thirty percent.

"Wow! That's still really impressive," Sara allows. "But you could have finished the whole thing—if you wanted to?"

"Yeah, I could have kept doing the same thing for another hundred days," I confirm.

I see the look on Noah's face, but he doesn't voice his disdain at my failed attempt or my nonchalant claim about being able to finish. He doesn't ask why I didn't finish, and I don't explain.

We stay up chatting until the sun starts to sink behind the trees and the mosquitoes' incessant biting drives us to shelter in our tents. They are hiking only a few miles farther than me the next day, and we arrange to see each other out of camp in the morning. Back in my tent, I stare at my Wilderness Trip Planner Map for twenty minutes before falling asleep. The map may not offer enough detailed information for me to truly dread the miles ahead, but the tiny numbers indicating distance between points of interest really seem to add up: 1.6 + 1.4 + 3.5 + 2.0 + 1.3 + 1.3.

11.1 miles.

Chapter 5

AT SOME POINT OVER THE YEAR AND A HALF I TOOK TO PREPARE for the Appalachian Trail, my parents resigned themselves to my confusing ambition. My mom agreed to handle my food drops so I wouldn't starve. My dad decided not to try to tell me what to do so he could keep his head from exploding. These concessions were equally ambitious and led to countless tense moments around the house in the weeks leading up to my departure. I ordered bulk boxes of single-serve raspberry jam packets and came home with backpacks full of Knorr rice sides. My father pressed his lips together in silent forbearing, opting to say nothing for lack of something nice to say. My mother and I organized a resupply shelving system in the laundry room with items sorted by category—cookies, bars, oatmeal—and a chart of post offices and mileage along the trail.

I purchased a Greyhound bus ticket from Little Rock to Memphis to Nashville to Atlanta and scheduled a hiker shuttle from Atlanta to Amicalola Falls. The bus ride would take sixteen hours but cost considerably less than a direct flight. After quitting my job for the journey, I had an abundance of time on my hands and a limited supply of cash. I had never ridden on a transit bus before and was nervous. I told myself that a strong independent woman who hikes alone can definitely use public transportation alone.

The day before I was scheduled to leave, a snow and ice storm blew through Little Rock headed east. I stood at the front window looking out at a steely gray sky and wrung my hands. I worried that the bus would be canceled. Not as much as I worried that it wouldn't be, and I would have to start my hike in bad weather. I didn't know if I was tough enough to hike in an ice storm. But I certainly wouldn't be able to quit. The Appalachian Trail was the only thing I had talked about for over a year. My reputation was at stake.

Luckily, the bus was canceled, allowing me a reprieve from my doubts. I rescheduled my start date, postponing two whole weeks. Two more weeks in the comfort of my parents' house, warmed by central heating and chilled by the uncomfortable silence of disapproving parents and a young woman trying to hide her sheer delight in breaking away from their lifelong script.

On the morning I left, I carefully placed six days' worth of food in the top of my pack and clipped the lid down on a full load for the first time. When I slung the forty-pound burden over my shoulder, I lurched under the weight. I hid my surprise as I carried it purposefully out to the driveway and deposited it in the backseat. My father drove in silence and my mother sat blankly in the passenger seat.

As we pulled into the parking lot, mom turned back and smiled through the pain.

"Be good, be careful," she said.

I had heard those words a thousand times before. It was a wise motherly proverb—always reminding me that my safety was my own responsibility. As if to be good and careful were one in the same and the key to success in a dangerous world.

I came around to the front seat and hugged her so she wouldn't have to get out of the car. The chemotherapy and radiation had left her with low energy, hardly able to walk from one room to another without rest. She was showing definite improvement after a particularly rough round of treatment. It hadn't seemed likely two weeks before that she would be able to tolerate the car ride to see me off. Because of the ice storm, I got to say goodbye to my parents together. Somehow, it made me feel better—more confident, more prepared, more supported.

Dad came around and lifted my pack, hiding his emotions under a comical staggering and huffing and puffing. He helped me into the straps. I gave him an eye-roll laugh, the kind he had come to know too well through the years. The same I had given every time he replied to requests such as "Daddy, will you make me a sandwich?" with "abra-cadabra, you're a sandwich."

"I love you, Daddy." I rested my head on his shoulder as he wrapped his arms awkwardly around my pack. Memories of hugging him goodbye as a small girl flooded my brain, pressing my face into the stomach of his starchy uniform shirts. I struggled to compose myself as the significance of my change in height crashed against the implication of our role reversal. For the first time, I was leaving him at home. He would be the one waiting days between phone calls, hoping I was safe but not knowing for sure.

With that, I turned and walked into the station. The smell of fuel hung in the air as I waited for the bus. I had spent the last year telling myself that this was the moment I would leave my old life behind. The new me was strong, independent, and fearless. But in that crowded, noisy bus station my nerves got the better of me. I watched warily as people around me went about their lives, wondering if any of them meant me harm. I wasn't walking confidently into the unknown. I still carried the fear that had been so lovingly ingrained in me. I was a girl traveling alone, and that was a dangerous thing to do.

––––––

On my fourth day on the Appalachian Trail, I hiked nine miles. I had spent the previous night snuggled up with a cute guy named Dirt. A rite of passage on the Appalachian Trail is to receive a trail name for doing something unique, cool, or stupid. When we met, I was impressed that he had acquired one so quickly. Come to find out it wasn't so much a trail name as it was a nickname from his regular life. Dirt was hiking with his best friends from high school, a young couple, and it seemed like he was accustomed to the third wheel arrangement. They welcomed me in, and I instantly felt like part of a crew. Even though I had wanted to strike out on my own, part of what I hoped to find was my people. And maybe my people went by names like Dirt.

The air was thick and sweltering and my hair hung in two heavy braids in front of my shoulders. I might have considered cutting it before the trail, to lose a few easy pounds, but I couldn't let my mom down in that way. When I woke each morning in my tent, I tied it into braids. They were never as sleek or tight as she could make them. But I could feel her fingers deftly pulling each strand into place.

My new friends all carried ridiculously heavy packs. Loaded down with military MREs and gear designed for leisurely car camping, they inched slowly up the steep trail. My pack was considerably lighter, so I tried not to look like

I was struggling as the miles dragged on, even as the sweat ran down my back and my legs turned to jelly. Early in the morning, rumors were swirling about trail magic at Gooch Gap, nine miles away. We took fantastic guesses at what was in store.

Trail magic is an integral part of thru-hiker culture. Past hikers and lovers of the trail set up at road crossings with goodies for tired hikers. I had read many stories of hikers famished and stumbling, thinking about giving up and going home. Just as they were preparing to hitch a ride straight to the airport from the next road crossing, they came across a couple of angels grilling up hamburgers and serving cold beers. Many tales of completed hikes give all the credit to the day trail magic kept them going.

We reached Gooch Gap in the early afternoon despite our sluggish pace. There were at least a dozen tents set up among the trees and several trucks pulled to the side of the road. Folding tables and chairs were arranged around a huge pot of chili and hikers moseyed around in their socks and crocs, holding sodas and talking trail. Some people had started their hike only the day before and still seemed freshly showered. Some looked and smelled as if they had skipped a few showers before starting, for good measure. Dirt and I went to stake out a flat piece of ground. I was starting to find a rhythm in making camp, setting up my little tent, blowing up my sleeping pad and fluffing my down sleeping bag.

I hadn't turned my phone on all day—reception was spotty and searching for a signal was a sure way to end up with a dead battery in an emergency. In between taking off my heavy boots and joining the others in line for chili, I held down the power button and stuck the phone in my back pocket. As I scooped chili out of the pot, my phone vibrated.

Over and over—too many times. I set my bowl down on the table and pulled the phone out to check.

Each of my dad's texts urged me to call immediately, find a way home, call as soon as I get this. As I scrolled through the list of notifications, everything else fell away. I was no longer standing in a crowd of dirty hikers, no longer hanging out with my new friends, no longer about to dig into a hot bowl of magic chili. I stared at the screen, paralyzed by the implication of such a string of pleading communication— why would he send message after message to no response? It was as if he thought I wasn't answering due to a lack of understanding of the gravity of the moment. Or maybe it was comforting to him to be able to say he was still trying— trying to get through, the messages piling up behind my blank screen, waiting to get out.

I asked a trail angel to drive me to Atlanta, and like a true angel, she saved me. I called my father to tell him I was on my way, he said mom was already gone. In the airport, I cried alone in a rigid plastic chair. Would I have done something differently if I had known that the last time I would see my mom would be in the parking lot of that Greyhound bus station? Our goodbye felt self-centered now—the weight of it solely derived from the coming-of-age, life changing story I intended to live out over the next six months. I had taken for granted that she would be there when I returned home. She was gone, and I was alone. Not the kind of alone one elects to undergo when hiking through the woods without a partner, but the kind of alone into which one is thrust when they lose their sense of self by losing the one person they could be defined by. Without my mom, who was I?

———

In the days that followed, I stared blankly into space while family members filtered in and out of my parents' house. This place used to be filled with family, and now it was filled with strangers. Relatives I considered distant spoke to me like we were close. On the day of the memorial service, an uncle I hadn't seen or spoken to in nearly a decade posed a question which struck me as insensitive and insane.

"So, when are you going to go back out on the trail?"

I blinked and scrunched my face. My brain muddled through the question one word at a time. When? Who could think about the future at a time like this? Linear progression of time had ceased entirely, and he wanted me to make plans for the future. I couldn't go back on the trail, I had familial duties to tend to. People would be expecting me to do things. Things you do when your mother dies. I hoped someone would tell me what those things were so I could start doing them.

But could I go back? My dad hadn't wanted me to go before, he couldn't possibly be fine with it now. I looked around at the photos of my mother sitting on every surface in the room. Somehow, in that moment more than ever, I needed to hike. I needed to push myself, to use my body, to know I was capable.

In her death, I saw the bleak end of a road I had been desperately trying to veer away from. Taylor's words rang again in my ears. He had been worried I would turn out like my mother. I didn't want to end up like her either. She was gone too soon.

"I don't know," I replied vaguely and wandered away. I spent the better part of the day moving from room to room any time someone looked like they might be ready to speak to me, eventually escaping to the master bedroom and falling asleep in my father's bed in the middle of the afternoon. The house felt empty again—but it wasn't my own loneliness that expanded to fill the space this time. There was hardly room for my sorrow, my father's pain had grown to 3,000 square feet. It filled every nook and cranny; it permeated the rooms we never entered and settled around the dishes in the cabinets.

———

In the following days, I realized that my face, so much like my mother's, was more of a painful reminder than a comfort to my father. The second time he called me by her name, I started to think about going back to the trail.

I stepped back on the Appalachian Trail at Gooch Gap only ten days after I had left. It felt as if a whole lifetime had passed since I had last seen this place, and in some sense, it had. There was no trail magic that day. The sky was dreary, and a chill hung in the air. I hopped from the shuttle and, without much pretense, headed north. It was fortunate the trail left nothing to the imagination: walk north, stop when you are hungry, stop when you are tired, continue north.

The next few days passed blankly. I walked alone and set up my tent close enough to shelters to ensure my safety among dozens of other hikers but far enough away that I didn't meet them. My mind was empty, each sound of the trail entering through my ears and echoing hollowly in my head until a new sound came along. I had no thoughts for days on end, only the reverberation of my surroundings.

A week or so later, I walked eight miles in the rain. My clothes were soaked, and my skin stung with the cold. It occurred to me that this was a particularly difficult day, but only objectively. To me, it was no different than the other days I had had since coming back to the trail. I noticed other hikers taking breaks—they sheltered under rock outcroppings to eat their snacks and hang out, reminding themselves this was supposed to be fun. I trudged by, peering out from beneath the low hood of my obscenely bright turquoise rain shell and sloshing through deep mud puddles, placing my feet deliberately on the trail to avoid losing my footing in the thick slop. When I reached the shelter, it was packed, and tiny tents surrounded the modest structure. I searched for a flat spot to claim and planted myself a hundred yards uphill from the main gathering area.

I dug my food bag and camp stove out of my pack and headed down the hill to prepare my dinner. The one picnic table was occupied by a group of boisterous hikers dressed in either $2 ponchos or $200 rain jackets. They compared stories from the day's walk and discussed their mileage thus far. I cringed at the idea of sitting down with the group and hung my bear bag without eating. When I got back to my tent, I curled up in my sleeping bag and turned on my phone. I had a strong signal and scrolled through my messages, trying to decide who to contact. I wanted to feel connected, to know somebody cared about my day. I read each name on the list. No, not them. They were too busy. They had their own life to think about. They didn't want to hear about my day. They would want to talk about my mom. They would be worried I would want to talk about my mom.

In that moment, I knew the person who cared about my day was the very person who would never again be available to call. I could never again pick up the phone with nothing more interesting to relay than, "it rained today, and it's cold, and I miss you." A mom cares about these details—perhaps a partner would care about these details. I turned my phone off and fell asleep.

Day 5: August 6, 2018
Pyramid Creek → Snow Lake

FOR THREE MILES, THE TRAIL BETWEEN PYRAMID CREEK AND Longmire descends steeply. My nearly empty food bag is light in my pack. Picking up my first food cache today signifies the completion of one third of my journey. The past four days have been grueling at times. I've questioned my desire to be on this trip and whether backpacking is even meant to be fun. Now I feel a glimmer of accomplishment and can hardly imagine not completing the trail. I give myself a pat on the back for sticking with it.

There are more people on this three-mile stretch than any other part of the trail so far. I cross several groups of hikers setting out from Longmire on their first day of a thru-hike. They're fresh and enthusiastic and only have one question in mind.

"Have you seen any bears?" they ask.

I repeatedly assure strangers I haven't seen a bear, although there is a rumor of one in the Golden Lakes area. People's fascination with the imagined threat of bears is perplexing, compared to their total lack of concern about other, more pressing dangers.

After talking to a group of four, I wonder, for the first time, how I look and smell. The unpleasant chemical aromas of deodorant and hair products waft from them. Harsh artificial scents are abrasive to my brain after days of taking in trees and wildflowers and natural human smells. Long after we part ways, I can hear a steady flow of conversation until they're out of earshot.

Just as I'm able to focus in again on the rustling of leaves and the movement of critters in the bushes, my reverie is interrupted by the sounds of cars passing on a nearby road. I skip with joy; three miles have passed easily and I'm back in civilization. I hurry past the ranger station and into the gift shop first, dropping my pack on the porch on the way in. Candy and baked goods and ice cream and ramen packets line the shelves. For some reason nothing seems appealing, perhaps it's all too overwhelming. In the overpriced camping essentials section, I grab a pack of dental floss and hunt around for toilet paper without success.

Sara and Noah are dubious when I come out of the store with nothing but dental floss. They sit happily on the porch with ice cream bars in one hand and sodas in the other.

"They don't sell toilet paper here!" I exclaim. "Now I'm forced to steal some out of the women's restroom, when I was totally willing to pay money for it."

Their laughter fades behind me as I march off to the women's restroom. I cram a wad of toilet paper into the quart size Ziploc containing the dwindling roll I brought with me.

At the Longmire Ranger Station, my food cache awaits. I ask the ranger if I can put some things back into my plastic tote and pick them up at the end of my hike. As with any backpacking trip, I have packed unnecessary silliness. Only a few days of walking have revealed the error of my ways.

I unload the bin into my food bag and toss one of the dinner-for-breakfasts back. Mashed potatoes with freeze dried broccoli and wild jungle peanuts with no seasoning was a terrible miscalculation. It's thick and flavorless and impossible to swallow and I will *not* start another day that way. The Ranger Station has a hiker box in the corner through which I rummage for a replacement. Hiker boxes are designed for backpackers to exchange items: the take-a-penny, leave-a-penny of thru-hiking. They're often filled with oatmeal packets and unlabeled mystery baggies of home-dehydrated whose-its and whats-its. There is nothing dinner-like to replace my mashed potatoes. I do score several bags of jellybeans, sorted by color, and one of granola with large pieces of dried fruit which looks promising.

I inhale the bag of green jellybeans (watermelon, apple, and … margarita?) as I unload and reload my pack, meticulously evaluating the practicality of each item within. I ditch my hiking shorts (my long pants can easily be rolled up), my down jacket (I've only worn it once), and my sunscreen (I have a solid base tan from spending the last three months outdoors). In evaluating each item I have brought along, I must ask myself if the possibility of needing it is worth the weight on my back.

In backpacking, the weight of what you carry is physical. In life, the weight of what we carry isn't so corporeal. I carry the promise to myself not to let another man treat me badly. I carry the responsibility to guard myself and never show vulnerability. I carry the promise to never cause someone pain by leaving them behind. I've been carrying these weights for some time. Am I willing to continue carrying that trauma? That grief? That anger? Is there a time that it may come in handy? Perhaps I could move forward more quickly—or easily—if I set it down.

———

My stomach growls as I cross the parking lot and step inside the National Park Inn. The lobby of the hotel is rustic and sparse, with only one employee sitting behind a desk between a plain wooden staircase and the entrance to the dining room. A woman in her fifties with a severe looking blonde bob and far too much makeup greets me as I walk in.

The dining room is nearly empty, and nobody appears to be playing the role of hostess, so I turn to the woman behind the desk.

"Can I get a table?" I ask.

She rises from her post and comes around the desk. "Follow me."

The flowery chemical smell of her perfume creates a tunnel through the room. It would be just as easy to follow her with my eyes closed.

The server comes over with a glass of water and straw in hand. She and the only other server in the room are both middle-aged blonde women, same as the woman working in the lobby. After taking my order, she walks off with the menu. I quickly wish she'd left it behind so I would have something to look at. Without a cell phone or a companion, I am left to sip water and look alternately between the two photos on the wall adjacent to me and the three others across the dining room; although these are hard to make out at such a distance and give me the look of someone staring into blank space. All the photos are of Mt. Rainier, and once given a cursory glance, they don't offer much of interest to the casual consumer of photography.

There's a family sitting several tables over and they're

putting on quite a show. I find it difficult to observe them without being too obvious. Although, it would hardly seem possible to sit alone in an otherwise silent room to do anything else. Once I've received my orange juice, I wage an inner battle between drinking the juice to give me something to do and trying to conserve it so there will be some left by the time my food arrives.

My eyes squint shut every time one of the two servers moves through the room yelling "CORNER" at the top of their voices, as if they're working in a bustling establishment with narrow walkways and other staff whizzing around blind corners carrying trays brimming with full beverages and hot plates. That is clearly not here. This is where old servers go to semi-retire, serving lazy breakfasts to nearly empty rooms in the shadow of a looming Mt. Rainier.

I sip orange juice. Mrs. Family Mom shushes Little Miss Two-Year-Old as she screams relentlessly. Helpful Miss Six-Year-Old coos loudly to the toddler, practicing her soothing mom routine and offering her little sister a crayon. I sip water. Mr. Family Dad attempts to engage Middle Miss Four-Year-Old about the coloring place mat she is waving around, almost pleading with her to continue drawing rather than adding to the cacophony.

"Did you color in the bear? What is that one? A marmot?"

I sip orange juice. I wonder how long they have been sitting there, as I've rarely seen a table so hectic unless their food is seriously delayed.

The other blonde, middle-aged server appears from the kitchen with a small dish and hustles over to the table. I sip water.

"Here's a scrambled egg for the little one!" she chirps with a false cheer which hardly disguises the desperation of a server who is fully aware their tip is going to hell in a handbasket.

Mrs. Family Mom doesn't have time to express gratitude as she snatches the plate of egg and offers it to her youngest child. "Eggs, you want some eggs."

The little girl opens her mouth expectantly, no sound coming out for the first time, and the mom shovels some scrambled eggs in.

"That's the ticket." The server lets out the most outrageous laugh; two long, loud, nasally "HAAAA"s.

I snort into my orange juice. The miraculous arrival of one scrambled egg has nearly silenced the table. Mrs. Family Mom and Helpful Miss Six-Year-Old no longer have a screaming toddler to loudly quiet, and the dining room is suddenly a bit more peaceful. I look over at the nearest photo of Mt. Rainier. Minutes crawl by.

The egg is gone. Little Miss Two-Year-Old is quickly deteriorating, and her volume is escalating. Mrs. Family Mom is waving over their server, asking if they could order another scrambled egg. I sip orange juice. Chaos ensues.

Middle Miss Four-Year-Old has vacated her seat and is now doing laps around the table tapping her younger sister on the head each time she passes. No Longer Trying to be Helpful Miss Six-Year-Old has taken over the coloring sheet and is pointing at the animals and yelling their names into the room. "BEAR! MARMOT! DEER! MOUSE!"

Mrs. Exhausted Mom rises from her seat and takes her youngest out of the room, leaving Mr. Family Dad to wrangle the other two.

Within a few minutes, relative calm returns, the girls have settled into their seats, and Mr. Family Dad sighs deeply. Mrs. Family Mom returns alone, causing me to wonder where one might abandon a screaming child in a classy establishment such as this. Without the loudest of their progeny, Mom and Dad are able to start an actual conversation.

"You know, I think that book, *Wild*, is about this place."

"Oh, is that Pacific... Pacific Trail here?"

"Yeah, I think so."

"You know it goes all the way into Mexico?"

"There's other ones too, like on the East Coast. The Appalachian Trail, I think."

My ears perk up.

"Oh yeah, but that one's supposed to be way easier, the mountains out here are much bigger."

I give my best side eye to the room at large. I could see how a non-backpacker might fall for this logic. The amount of elevation gain vs miles of trail is significantly greater on the Appalachian Trail, even as the highest elevation is hardly impressive compared to the Pacific Crest Trail. The couple discusses long-distance backpacking as a foreign concept; something to write books about, a grand illusory adventure not intended for mere mortals. It can be easy to forget, now that I am immersed in the culture of backpacking, that it wasn't long ago that I knew nothing of these things either.

I consider their lives—the parents of three small girls, with priorities like feeding and clothing them. They could probably describe ad nauseum the merits of their school district and other things which are of little interest to me. They fill their minds with the concerns of a life I have thus far opted out of.

I try to picture myself as a mother, wrangling three squealing girls while maintaining some semblance of an adult relationship with a partner. How did my parents do it? They stayed so impossibly in love over the years. If you ask my father about their marriage, they had two fights. Two! I wasn't there for either of those, therefore I'm convinced it's their fault I have such a low threshold for disagreement in my romantic endeavors. I was raised in a fairy tale house. I wasn't only given false ideas about love and relationships by Cinderella and Ariel, but it seems that my own family set an outrageous standard.

Sometime in the last ten years, I stopped thinking about having children of my own. Recently, I've started to recognize that the parents I see are often my age or younger. I do sometimes catch myself imagining a tiny me running around with a snotty nose and no front teeth. The thought occasionally slips in that at twenty-eight years old, it isn't too late to change my mind. I'm still trying to figure out what I'm about in this world, and the responsibility for another human life would derail a journey that's only just begun. Besides, I don't have a partner anyway.

The server stops by to fill my glass and let me know my food will be right out. She's not convincing. I sip orange juice. I estimate that forty-five minutes of my life have now passed in this dining room.

When breakfast finally arrives, I'm equal parts ravenous and disinterested. I inconspicuously stuff my face with an entirely unremarkable eggs benedict and pay my check. By the time I walk out, the family at the other table is mercifully being served.

Back on the trail, the moisture in the air attaches itself to me as I press onward and upward. The three and a half miles from Longmire to Paradise River Campground climbs steadily, gaining over 1,000 feet of elevation. Paradise River Campground is closed for the season. The unavailability of these four campsites has caused my strange itinerary—two miles one day and almost eleven the next. The signs posted at Paradise River indicate the area has been shut down due to dangerous trees that are at risk of falling. I remember hearing stories about hikers on the AT camping under "widow-makers" and being crushed to death in the night. I circumvent the warning signs to have a look around; the campsites are nothing to write home about, and the trees in question do look fairly treacherous.

Less than a mile from the campground is a crowded side trail to Narada Falls. The hike from Longmire is almost four miles, so surely all these people haven't come that way. The sympathetic looks they give make me think I must look like hell—sweaty and red-faced from the perpetual incline. My shoulders ache under the new weight of my pack. I badly want to breeze by the falls without taking the 0.2-mile detour to the viewpoint but am assured the short walk is worth it. My feet hurt. My back hurts. I still have three or four miles to go. I don't even care about this waterfall, but it's not like I'm going to come back to see it another time.

Less than five minutes later, I stand before the falls. Not the most spectacular waterfall I've seen, even on this trip, still I shake my head at the desire to forego a view to save myself five minutes of effort. So lazy. The power and majesty of moving water always ignites something within me. There is a human instinct to admire water in its many forms—it is essential to life—but I feel more of a kinship than utility when I stare into its depths.

I stop to reference the Wilderness Trip Planner Map, even though Narada Falls isn't marked on it. Reflection Lakes is about a half mile away, the map shows a group of three lakes. Hopefully they're decently sized for a swim.

Struggling through the heat of the day to the height of the ascent, I fantasize about stripping down to my underwear and jumping in the lakes.

Much to my chagrin, the trail emerges from tree cover along a busy road and I find myself standing between Reflection Lakes and a parking lot. Dozens of tourists wander this way and that on the sidewalk. So much for diving in. True to the name, the first lake offers a perfectly reflected view of Mt. Rainier. I hadn't noticed that the Wonderland Trail joins with a road right before reaching the lakes. This disappointment could easily have been avoided with more attentive map reading.

With shoulders hunching and head hanging, I push through the throngs. On the other side, I detour from the Wonderland Trail to Snow Lake, a camp with only two sites which could hardly be considered "back-country" as it's only one mile from a parking lot. I'm staring at my feet as I navigate the rocky terrain, when an older man stops and asks if I'm staying the night.

"Yep," I answer honestly. Lying seems impossible, as I'm carrying a full backpack on a one-mile trail.

"Well the first campsite has the most amazing views, but the second has a little more privacy." His smile is good-natured, but my thoughts are running wild.

Oh good, he's familiar with the area. More privacy so weirdos can't find me? Or more privacy so nobody can see weirdos murdering me? Also, nobody asked for your two cents dude. Whoever said that young women alone needed advice from creepy old men on the trail? Maybe I'm being overly sensitive. Maybe this guy is just friendly and chatty and wants to share his insights—without considering whether I need or want them.

I glance back over my shoulder to make sure he's moving along, and he's already out of sight. At a fork in the road a signpost indicates: Snow Lake to the right, Snow Lake Camp to the left. A couple of teenage girls in jean shorts and Chuck Taylors are staring at their phones in the first campsite before the stunning backdrop of a snow-capped Unicorn Peak reflected in the glimmering surface of Snow Lake. The second campsite gives me the creeps, hidden deep in the trees.

The girls eventually wander back to the trail, so I pounce on the vacated first campsite. It's hardly big enough for a one-person tent, perched atop a rocky outcrop. The maximum allowed in an individual site is five, which couldn't possibly fit here.

I wasn't able to jump into Reflection Lakes because of the abundance of tourists crowding the area, but Snow Lake is much quieter. Several groups of hikers are scattered around the banks: some dipping their feet in the water, some not so bold. Site 1 is certainly not as private as I might like, but as I learned on the AT: there's no such thing as modesty on a thru-hike.

Yanking off my hiking pants and tank top, I stand tentatively on the large rock overhanging the lake. I only need to glance across the blue water to see the patch of snow stubbornly clinging to the north-facing side of Unicorn Peak during August's record-breaking heat wave. I squat down on the rock and dip my hands into the water. It's frigid, and just like that, the idea of jumping in has instantly lost its appeal.

I want to be the type of person who always jumps into an alpine lake when presented with the opportunity. The type of person who indulges the urge and embraces the shock to the system. Cold submersion is good for the body, and I've never regretted it in the past. There is nobody here to talk me into it, to coax me in or jump first and assure me the water is fine. I must do this myself—for myself and by myself.

I drop to my butt and dip my feet in the water, icy needles prick my skin, and the numbing comes shortly after. After several long days on the trail, the numbness is a reprieve from the constant aching in the soles of my feet. I push myself off the rock and stand on the lake bottom, the water rising above my knees. This too is uncomfortable for a moment, but soon it becomes bearable and almost pleasant. I wade out until the water is nearly up to my groin and I hesitate, knowing I should take the plunge in one swift move, dunking my more sensitive areas all at once or I'll never see it through.

The stickiness of dirt and sweat on my skin aren't bothersome enough to coax me beneath the surface. With eyes closed, I envision physical tendrils of warmth reaching down from the sun through miles of sky and caressing my shoulders and face. The sun will still be here to dry me after I jump, and I will be warm as soon as I get back on land. I ease further in, too slowly, the water is up to my waist and threatening to wet my sports bra. My entire body is locked tight as I hop back and forth on the tips of my toes. The bottom of the lake is uneven, and each step is uncertain. I scurry toward the bank with images of disastrous tripping and slipping in my head.

Regret. I'm unable to commit, unable to suck it up and do the thing. I am too weak to jump in cold water. Too afraid of a little discomfort.

I tug my fleece jacket over my sports bra and gather a few items of clothing to wash, most of which have been in constant use for five days now. A couple in their fifties sneak up behind me. They seem surprised to have stumbled into my camp, even having passed two signs along the way that clearly indicate campsites ahead and lake access the other direction.

The couple exude all-American mom and dad energy. His jean shorts and New Balance tennis shoes matched perfectly to her Mt Rainier crew-neck sweatshirt. Wringing the dirty water and biodegradable soap from my tank top, I welcome them to my temporary home.

In the years since losing my mother, I have found comfort in other people's parents. They fill a void in my life left by the complete lack of concern or disapproval I receive from my own father, who can hardly seem to muster the energy to even ask where I'm going when I tell him I'll be out of phone reception for the next twelve days. For this reason, I engage the couple and for this reason, I give them hell as if they are my own parents.

"Where are you guys from?" I start.

"Ohio, you?" Dad replies.

I'm acutely aware of my outfit: black bikini-style underwear and fleece jacket zipped over a sports bra. They seem unperturbed, and I feel uncharacteristically safe with them.

"Oh, Ohio! I've heard good things." I wink. "I come from Colorado most recently."

I leave the history at that, as the play-by-play of my nomadic past is hardly necessary for this interaction.

"Are you hiking the Wonderland Trail?" Mom asks.

It must be obvious by my laundry day antics—the only other possible explanation being that I live here.

"Yeah, I'm on my fifth day." I nod.

"Are you hiking by yourself?" Dad asks.

"Yep!" I tell them without a second thought.

"Aren't you afraid to be out here alone?" Mom asks.

Although the question is hardly original, the word 'alone' cuts a little deeper than usual.

"Afraid of what?!" I wince but shake it off with good humor and false naivete.

"Bears? Murderers?" Mom has got a pretty wild imagination.

"Wait. Are you guys going to murder me?" I try my best to look taken aback, as if the thought had never occurred to me before, and now I'm worried for my safety, in broad daylight, with Mr. and Mrs. American Heartland.

Mom gasps faintly. "No, we aren't going to murder you, but you never know what kind of weirdos are out in the woods." She gives me a stern look.

I rebut with the usual "You never know what kind of weirdos are in the city," and "I have never felt less safe on trail than in society," and "I have scheduled campsites for every night out here, so if I went missing, they would know exactly where to look."

In truth, this campsite is the first place I've felt uneasy: it's close to the road, day hikers keep wandering through, and the other site is still unoccupied which means I could end up here completely alone tonight. The standard responses and defenses come automatically. I would never go into the capital W Wilderness alone, but a well-traveled trail in a National Park is nothing to be worried about.

They seem unconvinced. I don't always know that I'm convinced either. They tell me about their twenty-four-year-old daughter who wants to hike the Appalachian Trail, and I assure them she should. The Appalachian Trail made me. I'm not sure if that makes them feel better or worse. What if their daughter is emboldened to start doing all kinds of dangerous hiking alone? Perhaps it's better to keep her sheltered and fearful. It's safer that way.

The couple moves along and time creeps on, the sun sinks a little lower in the sky, and my trepidation grows. The second camp spot is still unoccupied. I sit picking at the gelatinous bandage on my toe. It had been quite secure until my dip in Snow Lake. Now the sopping goop peels easily from my sort of clean foot, revealing the blister underneath. Although the bandage seems to have kept it protected over the last several days, it hasn't healed at all and must be covered again.

Once my clothes are dry, I clear up the area and move my party of one into the tent. I ought to avoid being seen alone this close to nightfall. I stare at the ceiling of my tent, too anxious to close my eyes.

Voices of men drift up the trail, my ears perk up, my body tenses. I cringe at the worry that floods me. I haven't even seen them; they could be perfectly nice. I detest the programming that I should be afraid and wary of men. I detest the idea that at any moment I could become a victim. What I detest the most is that my own life experience has only confirmed the fear I've been told to live with.

Frozen in place, I strain to hear as the men come back by on their way out. Must be just another pair of nosy day hikers. I try to read a bit more, but my breathing is uneven, and I listen for any sign of life on the outside. It's growing too dark inside the tent to make out the words on the page, so I lay the book down and close my eyes. Go to sleep, I tell myself. Call it an early night, get some rest. Don't freak out, everything will be fine. Being alone in the woods is the point, remember. It's a National Park, everything will be fine, nobody is going to mess with me here.

Burrowed deep in my sleeping bag with the hood pulled up around my ears, I'm surrounded by my fear. We are partners in the night, breathing life into one another. The adrenaline threatens to keep me awake all night and I squeeze my eyes shut defiantly. I've been good. And careful. That's really all a girl can do, right?

Chapter 6

MY FOREHEAD PRESSED INTO THE SMEARED WINDOW OF THE FREE hiker shuttle as the road wound through the hills back to Unicoi Gap. The driver from the seedy discount motel in Hiawassee, Georgia waved as he deposited a load of freshly washed hikers into a small parking lot to rejoin our fellows on the trail. The flowery chemical smell of the cheap motel laundry soap failed to disguise the sweat-saturated synthetic shirts and nylon pants which would never again be suitable for off-trail wear.

The other hikers I had shared a room with disappeared up the trail, unconcerned with sticking together. I felt nothing about their departure—it was too early in the game to get attached to strangers, and these people were not my people. The trail zigzagged steeply from the road up the side of Tray Mountain. Exposed to the sun and wind, the path was baked and dusty, in direct contradiction with the runny slop we had been marching through for the past seventy miles.

I hunched my shoulders and leaned heavily onto my trekking poles as I climbed up, up, up. My pack was newly filled with food from town and weighed substantially more than it had the day before. Even in early April, the sun and humidity were fierce; sweat dripped into my eyes, causing them to burn and tear up. After what felt like hours of toil, I heard another hiker approaching. I slowed and stepped off the trail to allow them to pass.

"Oh, no I'll stay behind." The girl smiled comfortably. I shrugged and continued upward.

She walked close behind me. Why would anyone want to follow at my snail's pace? She looked more fit than me—her hair was not dripping with sweat, her face was not red as a beet, and her posture did not call to mind the image of an evil witch living out her elder years looming over a cauldron of brewing potions in the forest.

My legs were wickedly heavy as I lifted them forward; my body even heavier when I pushed down into my feet. I stopped at the end of every switch back to gasp for air and wipe the sweat from my brow. She stopped too and wiped the non-existent sweat from her brow. We bonded over our burning calves and sore shoulders and I learned her trail name, Yellowstone. She told me about wanting to make sure to take time alone on the trail, to camp away from shelters and really explore her independence. I was impressed with this and wondered who she was before the trail. For me, being out here at all was a grand statement of my independence, and I couldn't imagine doing something so senselessly dangerous as camping alone along the trail.

She wanted to make it to Deep Gap, thirteen miles from where we had met—I had hiked mostly seven or eight mile days up to this point and didn't know if I was up for the trek. For some reason I wanted to stick with this girl, she was the first person I had met since returning to the trail that I didn't immediately want to get away from. As I struggled to put thirteen miles under my boots, she could have easily left me behind. Instead, we carried on like old friends.

We stood before the GA/NC State Line sign at Deep Gap and exchanged high fives. When she turned away to check out the camping area, I grimaced. My toes screamed to get out of my boots where they were cramped and raw. I deliberately unlaced each boot and dislodged them before slipping my swollen feet into my hideous yellow Crocs. After such a strenuous day, the task of feeding myself seemed a momentous one. Yellowstone bounded around camp, merrily setting up her tent and preparing her dinner. A meal of Clif bars and fruit leathers was all I could manage. Afterward, Yellowstone suggested we go find a tree to hang our bear bags.

I followed her into the woods, where we assessed dozens of trees for their bear bag potential. Most of the shelters to that point had been equipped with bear lines, allowing hikers to easily hang bags of food and other smelly things over twenty feet in the air and far out of reach of curious black bears. This was the first time either of us had attempted to hang a proper bear bag. Yellowstone picked a tree and—allowing she probably knew more about this than I did—I agreed it seemed like a fine tree.

She tied a piece of paracord around a rock and aimed for the chosen branch. She hurled the rock high above us, missing the branch entirely. She picked it right back up for another try. She threw again and again, getting closer with some throws and totally blowing it on others. We doubled over in peals of laughter between throws. This girl was a shining example of the strong, independent, outdoor adventure woman I longed to be. In that moment, I realized she was still figuring things out too.

Thirty-five miles and a few days later, I found myself sitting in a bar restaurant in Franklin, North Carolina. We were a table of twelve, celebrating a stranger's birthday. It was April 15th, and in the other world people would be filing their taxes and thinking about money. The waitress brought trays full of pint glasses and shots. I hoped nobody noticed I only drank water.

A rather abrasive woman sat next to me, and I used her loudness as a shield—who could possibly see I wasn't participating in the festivities with her booming voice going a mile a minute? Throughout the evening I blended into the cushions of the corner booth, my mind buzzing with the activity.

An attractive young man sat on the other side of my shield and I watched him from behind my curtain of hair, released from its braids for the jaunt into town. He was thin—a runner for sure—with prominent angular features and a wide radiant grin. He was animated, and his laugh rang out across the table. Over the din of the bar, it was an enchanting sound. His trail name was Karaoke and the stories of his singing performances on the trail were perfectly suited to his energy at the table.

Every time I glanced his way, he seemed to be watching me with rapt attention and when our eyes met, he didn't look away. He was somehow participating convincingly in the group dynamics while trying to send me a covert message across the table. Was it possible I was imagining his attention? Wishful thinking perhaps. A man had never looked at me that way, with unabashed desire. I was not an object of desire. In the real world I was an ugly duckling, too lazy to put on makeup or style my hair, wearing baggy clothes to hide my pudgy belly and thick thighs, which combined with my impressive height never allowed me to feel particularly feminine or dainty.

Each time we locked eyes, it was electric—like waking from a month-long dream state and remembering I could connect to another human being. When we stood from the table, he was by my side as if by magic, and over the long walk back to the divey hiker motel we became acquainted. We stayed up late into the night with those of the group who weren't ready for bed. I kept wishing they would leave so we could be alone. We sneaked out to the patio and found some old lawn chairs overlooking the dirty parking lot.

There we delved into raw, intimate subjects and probed the most vulnerable parts we could find. I told him about losing my mom and how I had never experienced loss before; how I felt detached and guilty; how I questioned my decision to be on the trail at all. I told him I didn't feel like I could connect to other hikers because I didn't know how to have a normal conversation yet. Every time someone introduced themselves, I wanted to shout, "Hello! I'm Lady Unicorn and my mom just died." We shared a little bit of our pain, which made it feel a little bit lighter.

When we lay down in each other's arms in the wee hours of the morning, I felt safe and loved. When we hit the trail out of town with plans to meet up at a shelter that night, I felt hopeful and dreamy. When it became obvious in a few days' time I was not capable of matching his hiking pace and he decided to leave me behind on a rainy day, a new numb set in.

I sat in my soaked hiking clothes, weeping over the trail log where he had written to me. He requested that I camp there to allow him and his friends to move on to the next hostel. He thought a four-mile head start the next day may be enough to ditch me forever. I was not only devastated by the idea the spark I had felt was specious, but that I was being left behind because I couldn't physically keep up.

I was hiking the Appalachian Trail to redefine myself, to become the kind of woman who went hiking and enjoyed the outdoors, and that was the kind of man I wanted to be with. I hadn't conceived that my mere presence in the endeavor wasn't enough for miraculous reinvention. The long path toward becoming who I hoped to be didn't start and end by stepping onto the Appalachian Trail. It seemed there was more work to be done.

In the hours that followed, my sobs embodied the loss of Karaoke, the loss of my mother, my insecurity on this literal path, and my greater insecurity in attempting to become a woman I didn't know—a woman I had only imagined; a woman who was far greater than I felt capable of being.

"Are you okay?" A couple of older ladies approached the shelter.

I must have been a sorry sight, hugging my knees and crying while my clothes dripped an ever-larger puddle onto the floor. My shivers from the cold were indistinguishable from the shudders of sorrow wracking my body. One of the women touched my arm tenderly. I nodded and sniffled, unable to speak through my rigidly clenched jaw.

"Do you have dry clothes to change into?" The woman's face tightened with concern.

I nodded again.

"You should really put on something dry; you'll feel a lot better," she said.

There is a saying on the Appalachian Trail—*the trail provides*—and on that day, the trail provided me with a mom.

I don't remember her name or face, but I remember her maternal insistence that I get safely tucked in. Staying in a shelter for the first time, my sleeping bag lined up in a row of strangers, I listened to the rain continuing to fall and knew I would have to protect my heart better in the future. Like every broken heart, mine became rigid and hardened, more difficult to open the next time around.

In the following months, I spent most of my days walking alone, never staying long with other hikers. Occasionally, I found a friend whose pace matched my own, but socialization quickly became tedious and I invented excuses to hang back and let them go on without me. While groups of strangers came together into trail families around me, I checked out.

I managed to continually seem out of place, always being asked if I was a thru-hiker and repeatedly answering the question with some non-answer or other, "sort of" and "not really," all wrapped into one. I was no longer clear on what hiking the Appalachian Trail meant to me—my purpose lost in grief. The idea that I could be trying to prove myself or find meaning in life was drowned out by the glaring realization that life can be so much shorter than I had given it credit for. Maybe I didn't need to walk through the woods for six whole months.

The trail barely offered a distraction from my inner world. At each viewpoint I plodded past my fellow hikers and scoffed as they took in the wonders of nature. In the morning we all stood on one peak, looking toward the next one, and by mid-afternoon we stood atop that one and looked back at that from which we had come. Big whoop.

I met a man around my age who was carrying his father's ashes with him. This struck me as profoundly antithetical to my experience. Low Branch, named for his impressive height, was hiking in his father's honor, completing a journey they had often dreamed of doing together. His intention was so clearly defined, and he knew exactly how his father would have felt about it. My purpose seemed amorphous—I could never quite pin it down. When others suggested my mother would be proud of me, my stomach churned at their presumption. I longed to believe she would have been proud, but I felt her disapproval on my back, weighing me down like a forty-pound pack never could.

Seventy days into my hike, I strode into Pearisburg, Virginia—just another trail town stop. Referring to the map in my guidebook, I swung by the post office, picked up my food package and phoned my dad. I told him I was alive and asked him to send more food to the next town. I knew he'd never wanted this responsibility. My mom had been the one who reluctantly agreed to keep me fed on the trail. He didn't take the job seriously, sometimes sending five of the same dinner in a box. One week I ate nothing but red beans and rice. Without the prospect of choosing dinner, my thoughts had a little extra room on those days.

Those phone calls were always difficult, my guilt and his pain converging through the cellular static. That one felt different somehow and his quiet, strained voice echoed in my head as I trekked out of town. I marched through the swampy Virginia air, with sweat soaking my t-shirt and dripping from the tip of my nose. I tried to leave my worries behind, hoping they would fall off somewhere between mile 643 and mile 655.

By the time I reached the Captain's house, an unofficial campsite for AT hikers, I had already made up my mind. My fellow campers raided the back-porch refrigerator, downed free sodas, and delighted in the zip-line entry from the trail. Hiding from the mosquitos in the yard, I sat sweating in my tent and texted Lindy. *Do you know anyone that could give me a ride to the Roanoke airport?* It was time. I had told myself I would only hike as long as it felt like the right thing to do, and throughout the day I had come to realize it didn't anymore. I knew I could turn to Lindy, without having to answer difficult questions or explain my decision. She would never be disappointed in how far I didn't go. She knew how hard it could be.

The next morning, I dumped my food stores unceremoniously on the picnic table and offered my rations to the crowd. Under requisite pretense, they encouraged me to continue hiking and not give up. Most of them didn't know me, and I didn't deign to explain my reasoning to strangers. When they were assured that I was not to be swayed, they descended upon my meals and snacks like vultures.

Before noon, I said goodbye to the friends I had made and rode away from the Appalachian Trail. As I sat in another plastic chair at the airport in Roanoke, Virginia, I said goodbye to a dream. I had envisioned myself flying home from Maine in early fall, thin and tan, with more than 2,000 miles under my feet. I had pictured myself part of a family of thru-hikers, bonded forever by our shared achievement. More than anything, I had imagined I would be overcome by a sense of knowing, prepared to transition into some greater phase of life, some higher version of myself. This wasn't the end I had anticipated. This was not the victorious culmination of an empowering solo female journey. I was more lost and alone than ever before.

Day 6: August 7, 2018
Snow Lake → Nickel Creek

THE SUN PENETRATES THE WALLS OF MY TENT AND THE MORNING AIR has lost its cool by the time I rise. As it turned out, a couple of thirty-something gals arrived at the second campsite around eight o'clock last night. After ample time wrestling with my nerves, doubting myself and my security, I had the opportunity to stay up late socializing. The women are on a girls' trip and their version of backpacking is indulgent and fun: hike one mile (late in the day), carry luxury items, and stay comfy. I often think about what it would be like to backpack with a partner but usually my imaginary companion is a man—a love interest. These women reminded me for a moment that these are adventures I could share with a friend. The remedy to loneliness isn't always romance.

The chirping of birds and twinkling of Snow Lake are a beautiful distraction as I leisurely break camp. I know the ten miles to Nickel Creek will pass quickly, and I'll wish I had dawdled more. After eating, I leave my bright yellow and blue water bottle in the middle of the trail on the way to the privy to let my neighbors know it's occupied. The path to the toilet is straight uphill with no switchbacks, significantly steeper than any section of the Wonderland Trail. I use my hands to steady myself on the climb up to the privy in the sky. Anticipation builds for the magnificent view that must be at the top of such an unexpected climb. After all that huffing and puffing, there is nothing.

Perhaps the inconvenient location is intended solely for sake of privacy. The toilet itself is nothing more than a large plastic reservoir with a locking seat to deter curious critters from falling in. In theory, the lid would also discourage fly activity, but the swarm of black flies buzzing just below it seems to exist for the sole purpose of proving that theory wrong. I retch at the sheer number of flies released from the depths of the tank upon opening the hatch.

After a moment's hesitation, I wave my hands over the seat to shoo the flies away before taking the throne. As I sit, an old man bumbles out into the clearing, having followed the privy sign but not the privy signals.

"Uh... hello?" I greet the man. He jumps back with his hand over his mouth.

"Oh! I'm sorry! I'm sorry." His voice trails off as he all but runs back down the trail. I can hear him telling his companion, "It's open air!"

On my walk back down to the lake, I encounter the man and his wife. They have stopped to study my unaccompanied water bottle.

"Guess you didn't notice it there on your way up?" I muse as I collect the bottle.

"Oh, *that's* what that means!" he says.

———

About five miles after leaving Snow Lake, I arrive in Maple Creek campsite. Removing my boot and sock, I see that my new blister bandage is holding up well in the face of consistent downhill cramming. My detailed toe examination is interrupted by a man walking through the campsite.

He's wearing a military issue rucksack, camouflage pants, and boots that I have serious doubts anybody would voluntarily wear backpacking. His bright, round eyes peek out from under a gray bandanna tied around his forehead. He walks one way through the clearing and back the other way with a look on his face somewhere between confusion and indecision. He seems lost, which would be quite a feat in the middle of a well-marked campsite.

"Are you lost?" I ask.

"Uh... kind of?" he says, avoiding eye contact.

"Where are you headed?" I ask. This question has become a popular refrain in the last five days.

"Um, I was trying to make it to... Summerland today..." he answers slowly, as if he is pulling the idea from nowhere.

Johnny shifty-eyes over here. What's up with this dude?

"Oh, that's still pretty far." I exaggerate looking at my wrist where a watch would be, but I'm not wearing one.

"Yeah, what happens if I don't make it?" he asks.

He looks up at me and locks my eyes. His face is symmetrical, his jawline chiseled, his brow furrowed. I feel the heat rise in my cheeks and my stomach flip-flops. Objectively, he's incredibly attractive. His eyes betray a softness that contradicts his otherwise militaristic appearance.

Am I attracted to him? Well, he *is* the only man in the vicinity.

"They told me not to do something crazy to make my reservation, so it should be okay," I say. "Would you be able to catch up to your itinerary tomorrow?"

"Yeah..." He draws out the word. Obviously, I'm missing

something.

"I'm only going to Nickel Creek today. It would leave you pretty far from Summerland, but you're welcome to camp with me if you want," I offer.

"Can I do that?" He brightens at the suggestion.

"Sure, I have a campsite reserved, it's just me, there should be plenty of room," I say. "I'm Christine."

"Judah." He smiles and nods.

Certainly, he's carrying a weapon of some sort in his military getup, but I'm kind of sure he's not a murderer.

———

Judah follows me for the next two and a half miles; we're both sweating our way up the hill. I do my best to maintain a consistent pace and he does his best not to run me over. His stride is long in heavy soled boots and his breathing is loud but even. The greenery is ever present but not noteworthy; the trail is steep but not remarkably so.

I ask him about his gear. Why use military issue when such great lightweight backpacking gear is readily available? He explains that he's training for a promotion. Why anyone would want a promotion which requires tromping around with a heavy square pack on their back and clunky ill-fitting boots on their feet is beyond me. He's married, has a young son, and has spent nearly a decade in the military. He's looking at a significant promotion which will allow him to continue providing for his picture-perfect family. We have different priorities.

"Can I ask you something?" His reluctant voice suggests we are about to deviate from the three pillars of light backpacking conversation: gear, weather, and the next thing you plan on eating.

"Uh huh."

"I just worry about not being there for my kid, like this job is going to take me away from him even more and he's growing up so fast." It's more of a statement than a question.

"But isn't that the way of it?" I mull this over. "You have a child—you work your life away so your child can have better opportunities than you had. Then eventually they go off and work their life away, and maybe have a child of their own. What other option is there?"

"I guess..." Judah's voice trails off.

"The rat race is real, but my dad gave twenty-eight years of his life to the cause and he retired just in time for my mom to get diagnosed with cancer. He spent the first two years of his retirement taking care of her while she died. People think they're going to live their life when they're old, and some people don't make it. Now he's alone and has all the time in the world to dwell on how alone he is." I cringe at the nonchalance with which I tell this story. My parents' fate—reduced to a talking point.

"Wow, that is tragic," he mumbles, more to himself than to me.

I think about this man: he is somebody's father. There is a little boy out there who sees him as the smartest, most virtuous, best daddy in the world. And he's out here doing something for himself. I try to think of a time that my mom went and did something for herself. Not a single one comes to mind. I can't remember a time when she wasn't there, for even a day. From where I stood, she was always my mom, never Sally.

This is the reason I recoil at the idea of having children— the loss of my freedom. I can't imagine a world in which my mother would have left me as a toddler for a week or more just to do something for fun. She did her job diligently, never leaving my side. She watched over me and kept me safe, she told me that she loved me a dozen times a day. She cut my peanut butter and jelly sandwiches into triangles when I asked for triangles and rectangles when I asked for rectangles.

Somehow, I'm still angry at her for leaving me when she did. I feel betrayed by her promises. The promise she made to take care of me. The promise she made to love my father. I've kept myself from making promises to love anyone since she left. The surest way to avoid disappointing someone is not to let them expect anything from me.

———

When we reach the road crossing at Box Canyon, Judah and I run directly onto the stone bridge. There is only one car in the small parking lot by the Box Canyon sign.

"Do you know anything about this canyon?" I ask. "I've never even heard of it."

"Nope, I think it's only a lookout point for car tourists to stop and take a picture," Judah explains.

"Wow! This is SO cool!" I yell into the canyon with my body half-hanging over the stone wall. My voice disappears into the depths of the chasm.

Judah pulls out his phone and snaps a picture straight down where the river is flowing almost 200 feet below us.

"A picture doesn't capture it at all," he complains.

"My phone died days ago," I say. "It's actually been really nice. I've been able to experience everything without feeling like I need to try to capture it, put it in my pocket, take it home. Most pictures I take are disappointing to look at later anyway."

Judah stows his phone, and we stand for minutes staring into the gushing river. How did this specific area become such a deep and narrow canyon when others did not? We don't know. Side by side, we stand with our eyes closed. My whole body prickles to attention as the sound of the water echoes up between the narrow walls, distant but not faint. It's a symphony, each splash and gulp simultaneously emboldened and drowned out by those around it. The product is an undulating sonic wave whose individual components cannot be discerned.

Eventually we agree it's time to move on and continue up the trail. The next 300 feet of elevation pass without too much excitement, unless you include an enormous pile of feces in the middle of the trail. After thorough analysis, we conclude it could have been left by none other than a massive mountain lion. We exchange excited looks and waggling eyebrows at the idea that a mountain lion was recently standing where we now stand. Not just standing—shitting.

If I were hiking alone and came across such a large pile of scat obviously not left by a bear, I likely wouldn't expend the energy to decide where it must have come from. While it doesn't negate the fact that a mountain lion is in our midst, it's helpful to refrain from full-on panic when navigating the woods solo. I've always held that mountain lions are a non-issue. I spend no energy worrying about their presence or preventing their attack. If my destiny is to be eaten, then so be it. By the time I find out it will be too late, and there's not much I could do to prevent such an event anyway, so I've made peace with the possibility. The only way to avoid it would be to avoid any area where a mountain lion might be, and that's kind of a buzzkill.

———

We stroll into Nickel Creek campground well before sunset and pick out the prime campsite: plenty of space and a few trees perfect for Judah to set up his hammock. We've bonded throughout the day, and I'll be sad to see him go ahead tomorrow and leave me behind—a tale as old as time. We talk about his summit of Mt. Rainier the previous week over dinner. He shows me a picture of the rickety looking ice ladders he crossed on the mountain. On glaciated peaks, like Mt Rainier, ladders are often placed over deep crevasses and climbers balance on the rungs in their hiking boots and crampons. I've never seen anything like it.

"So, what's the deal with your hiking schedule? What do you need to do to get back on track?" I ask.

"What if, say, someone was hiking the Wonderland Trail without a permit?" Judah studies his bag of spaghetti and meatballs. "Would that be bad?"

"What do you mean, 'bad'?" I give him a pointed glare.

"Like would you care?" He peeks over to see my reaction.

"Of course I care! Why don't you have a permit!?" I try to look angry, but it's hard. We're friends now.

"Well, I wasn't sure I was going to be able to get this time off work, and I heard the permits are impossible to get, and I didn't want to try to get one and get turned down," he says.

"So, what's your plan? Try to make friends during the day and hide out in their campsites?" I jokingly accuse, as if he had somehow tricked me into inviting him to stay with me.

"Well, I was going to stealth camp with my hammock and hope nobody found me," he admits.

"What if they ask to see your permit?" I demand.

"Do they do that?" He grimaces, as if he hadn't considered the possibility.

"Yeah!" I say.

I'm assuming that's what they do!

"Well, I guess I'll deal with it when it happens?" he says.

"Well, if somebody asks to see your permit here, I don't know you. You're just some guy I picked up on the trail and I didn't know you were a fugitive." I work to keep a straight face.

"Deal." He cracks a smile. It's much better than the worried expression he'd been wearing.

Chapter 7

In the months that followed my time on the Appalachian Trail, my father and I watched eleven seasons of Grey's Anatomy. We sat on separate couches in a dark living room crying over every breakup, makeup, wedding, and fatal diagnosis. We cried extra when they talked about cancer and when the doctors stubbornly continued with CPR long past its viability. Before Mom's diagnosis, I had seen my father cry only once. During those months after her death, I often pretended not to notice his shoulders shaking while the tears flowed freely.

It didn't take long for my legs to begin to cramp up from the hours on the couch, and I knew I had to keep moving. I started to run. I hadn't run a single step since high school gym almost ten years ago, but I didn't know what else to do. Every morning before sunrise, I would step out into the thick August air. My lungs heaved with the effort before I'd gotten past the neighbor's driveway. My legs, having never quite adjusted to life on the trail, complained, and between difficult forty-five second jogging intervals I held the stitch in my side and gasped for breath.

I wore a pair of hideous teal and hot pink Nike's I had found in my mom's closet. They were a half-size too big for me but fairly new. As an avid collector of shoes, she must have felt they fulfilled some need, but I found them ironic. A token of fitness that neither she nor I possessed.

No matter how much or how often I ran, it could never take me far enough. I made circles through the cookie cutter neighborhood, always ending back at my father's door, always standing for an extra moment in the driveway, bracing myself for another day. Every day the same as the one before, replaying in my mind like deja-vu. I didn't belong here. As summer gave way to fall, running around the neighborhood turned into running across the country. I was drowning in my father's grief, and the only way out was west.

———

When I arrived in Denver the last week of October, I was surprised to find a cool breeze cutting through warm, sunny days. I planned to stay for a few days on the floor of Laura's tiny apartment. We hadn't seen each other since my trip back from Yosemite. I wanted to see the sights and get to know her new husband, Andrew, before continuing west through Utah, California, Oregon, and Washington, looking for a home. My mind was set on Portland, a city known for its weirdness and its gray disposition, which felt singularly appropriate. Despite my plans, I fell in love with the promise of Colorado.

Here was a place rife with possibility. From the middle of the bustling city, the view of the Rocky Mountains was something to behold. And within an hour one could stand atop the foothills and take in the equally impressive view of the twinkling metropolitan lights at night. Denver is well known for its 300 days of sunshine and for being one of the healthiest and most active cities in the country. It's jokingly referred to by the locals as Men-ver—a place where rugged active men come to pursue their athletic passions. It seemed like the perfect place for me to solidify my new identity and find a man to go along with it. The October sunshine was getting to me when Laura and Andrew suggested I stick around; at a time when I felt particularly lacking in connection and community, it was nice to be wanted.

I got a job and an apartment. From the outside, my new life may have looked eerily similar to the one I'd run away from when I started hiking the Appalachian Trail. The difference was me. On the other side of that adventure, I was not the person I had been before.

When Lindy moved to Denver, I had a partner in crime. We spent long evenings in our tiny apartment recounting our dating escapades, fueled by online match-making sites. We had weekly game nights and family dinners with Laura and Andrew where we laughed until our stomachs hurt and ate ice cream to make them feel better. It was like being back in Yosemite. For the first time in a long time, I didn't feel alone.

Lindy introduced me to the idea of polyamory. At first, I thought it was wild and offbeat—something I was theoretically but not practically interested in. Then I met Keith. We matched on an app and texted about our lives; he was funny and charming, and his pictures were cute in a goofy way. He was tall and fit and had shaggy ginger hair. He told me I didn't seem like the kind of girl who goes to dinner and a movie. He was right. When he asked for suggestions, I said let's do something intimate—something bold. He bought a couple's massage session, and we set a date.

When we showed up for our massage, we realized it

wasn't the kind of couples massage we had pictured. Rather than laying side by side and receiving matching massages, we were taking a massage lesson. A lesson in which we learned to massage each other. Talk about intimate!

Over the following weeks, I learned more about him than the knots in his shoulders. He told me about the loss of his father and his desire to find deep partnership. We were both disenchanted with the surface interactions we were faced with in our day-to-day lives and looking for something more meaningful. He confessed that he was hoping to be polyamorous, and I stifled my surprise. I had only just started to learn about polyamory, and it kept coming up.

I resisted the idea. I had found this beautiful human and we seemed so well suited, yet he wanted to keep looking. This triggered feelings of inadequacy and jealousy. I talked it over with Lindy and realized that I could take this as an opportunity. An opportunity to try loving in a new way. After all, loving by the standard playbook had never seemed to work for me. Why not try a new approach? So, I agreed.

If I could love and be loved by more than one person, I would never feel lonely. I could expand and grow, sharing myself with the world in a way most people can't even fathom. More importantly, I would never be anyone's world. I would always have the option to leave without the overwhelming guilt of breaking someone's heart. The idea allowed a freedom I hadn't imagined was possible.

I continued to swipe and match and date. I met a few other people I liked, and while most of them were receptive to non-monogamy, none were experienced with it. I struggled to establish meaningful relationships as these men seemed to perceive non-monogamous as casual. I needed to find someone who knew what they were doing.

On a cold January evening, Keith and I walked into a party like nothing I had heard of or experienced before. The house was chic, a place I could never imagine affording. A larger than life goddess statue made of tiny square mirrors welcomed us into the main living room. We held each other's sweaty hands on the way in, displaying our partnership even though the evening wasn't about partnership in the traditional sense; rather expansion and exploration.

At the direction of the hostess we dropped our names in a fishbowl and headed into the home theater where the party was set to begin. Thirty or so adults lounged on cushions arranged on the tiered floor. I scanned the room, assessing the group. There were a few older folks, but largely the group was under forty and a fairly attractive bunch. One guy caught my eye, he was wearing pale turquoise slacks and unmistakably hand-knitted striped socks. He had thick dark hair and huge mutton chop sideburns which could only have been ironic. The hostess interrupted my inventory to welcome us and kick things off.

We proceeded around the room to tell the stories of our first kiss. The perfect ice breaker for a party all about kissing and being kissed. She passed out little pink and red tickets tied with a gold ribbon—each one reading directives like "eat something off my body"—as a way to start an interaction with an appealing stranger, and suggested we each visit the kissing bar in the next room where we could order our favorite kisses all night. Spin the Bottle would be in the living room off the kitchen, and Seven Minutes in Heaven would start in the cozily decorated closet under the stairs as soon as we dispersed.

As we left the theater, I clung to Keith's arm, wondering how to engage appropriately. He suggested we start with a drink. I had quit drinking years before, but it seemed harmless and perhaps even helpful to have one in such an atmosphere. We headed upstairs and were served the cocktail of the evening—some fruity number which didn't taste too much like the liquor that was definitely in it. I downed it and looked up at him expectantly. He valiantly carted me around for the first part of the night. We held hands as we checked out the kissing bar, where you could order long, slow, romantic kisses or push-me-up-against-the-wall-with-fiery-passion kisses from whatever cute guy or gal was on shift. We checked out the truth or dare Jenga game happening next door and wrote our secret desires on scraps of paper for a bowl in the kitchen.

I got another drink and scanned the kitchen for Sideburns as we headed into the living room to play spin the bottle. The humans circled around the bottle were all attractive and I could see myself kissing any of them willingly. As the bottle spun around, people took turns locking lips over the table. My face grew rosy and warm from the alcohol and the cheer, and I found myself loosening up. I was having fun and feeling less unsure so when Keith got up and left the group, I wasn't too worried about it.

Before I knew it, his empty seat was occupied again. I looked over to see Sideburns admiring me in close proximity. He leaned in and whispered in my ear, "I can sit here and wait until the bottle tells us to kiss, or we could go somewhere else and do what we want."

A devilish grin crept onto my face, and he grabbed my hand. We walked through the kitchen, grabbing another drink on the way, and I tripped over a step as we headed into a dark hallway. My drink spilled on the floor and we giggled as I slipped across the wet tile. He caught me before I fell and held me up against the wall. When I scanned my body to feel if anything was hurt, the only sensation that registered was his touch.

His warm lips pressed into mine, and I smiled into his mouth.

I spent the rest of the night flirting and kissing this stranger. He ran his fingertips softly up my arm, across my collarbone, around my neck. We laid next to each other on a couch and whispered about our lives, our hopes, our loves—and the party went on around us. We were lost in each other completely. At the end of the party, we exchanged numbers and went home with our respective partners.

Keith expressed his compersion at my love match and I fell more comfortably into his arms than ever before. I had been skeptical of compersion, the idea that you can experience true joy when witnessing another's enjoyment of something. Jealousy is so ingrained in monogamous culture as to seem inevitable.

———

Around this time, I reluctantly started calling myself a runner. I began training for my first half marathon, which meant four runs a week. Monday, Wednesday, and Friday, I woke before sunrise, pulled on the same pair of black sweatpants, the same long-sleeve wool base layer leftover from the Appalachian Trail, and a shiny new running jacket. With a wool headband covering my ears and thin running gloves to protect my fingers, I stepped out into the dark, frigid January mornings.

Some days, forcing myself out of the house into the cold was the hardest thing I could imagine doing. I didn't know any runners, and if I had, I wouldn't have wanted to run with them anyway. I plodded along at an embarrassing pace.

The clunky sounds of my footfalls were covered only by my desperate gasping for air. Running was a solo activity—sort of. My body was always there. Always weighing me down, holding me back, following me around.

As soon as I reached the running path, our battle began. My body was a total drama queen. Her heart lived in her throat and the pounding made her gag and struggle to breathe. She constantly complained that her legs were too heavy, but I thought maybe her muscles were just weak. I told her that things would get easier. She called me a fucking liar.

Lindy became my cheerleader. She didn't have any interest in joining me on my runs but would be lounging on the couch in her pajamas when I came back in at six in the morning.

The first time I ran four miles, I collapsed on the living room floor afterward. Laying on my back, staring at the ceiling, I listened to my lungs sucking in ragged broken pieces of air.

"Great. Now just do that three times in a row and this half marathon is in the bag. What have I gotten myself into?" I worried.

"Yay Christine! You can do anything." Lindy's silly enthusiasm made me laugh until I wheezed. I think she truly believed I could do anything.

The first time I ran ten miles, I stared into the mirror at the crystallized salt tracks on my face. They lead down my cheeks from the creases of my eyelids. I knew it was sweat, but it looked remarkably like a stream of tears. I plopped on the couch and peeled off my moist socks to discover a black toenail on my right foot. It didn't even hurt.

I planned to run a race in Little Rock, so I could visit my

dad at the same time. I carried the whisper of a wish that my dad would come see me race. That he would be proud of my accomplishment and want to stand at the finish line holding a tacky sign with my name on it. He didn't.

"Running is boring," he said.

"That's true."

"You know I hate big crowds," he continued.

"I know."

"Have fun though," he said.

"I will," I lied.

I drove myself downtown at six on the morning of the race and I ran. For thirteen miles through the streets of Little Rock, I ran. A persistent drizzling mist leaked down on me and ten thousand strangers. The gray sky lent a sense of separation from everyone around me. I didn't run with them. This was between me and my body. It was always about me and my body. I didn't have the capacity for another person when I was running.

When I crossed the finish line alone, I leaned my head down so a stranger could hang a hideously enormous glittery finisher's medal around my neck. It was candy themed, complete with a peppermint twist that swirled independent of the frame and made me dizzy when I looked at it. My skin prickled away the cold numbness as I turned the heat up in my car on the way back to my dad's house.

———

Weeks later, back in Denver, I stood before the bathroom mirror and examined myself. I had lost a few pounds during the months leading up to the race, but not much. My inner thighs still leaned in toward each other, flesh still hung stubbornly around my hips. All that training, all that time invested. And then it was over, just like that. I thought that finishing the race would mean I had won the battle. After everything I had done, I still looked at my body with distaste. My body looked back at me with nothing to say for itself.

Is it my body's fault? My relationship with Keith had transformed into platonic friendship. Sideburns had let me down easy on a blustery day, citing irreparable differences of intention. He had a loving primary relationship and outside of him, I had nothing. It wasn't a fair match. Even though I had expanded my definition of love I still couldn't seem to make anything fit. I had worked painstakingly to create some better version of myself and here I was—still no good. In trying to avoid real connection, I was the one who ended up hurt.

My reflection ran her hands through the hair that hung long on either side of my face and down to the middle of my back. It had been two years since my mother's death—four and a half since her diagnosis. The weight of my hair was a constant reminder of the tears she had wept as hers fell out in clumps. I slowly dragged her old plastic comb through my tangles and remembered her sitting behind me on the couch, pulling a brush through my hair.

My hair pulled on my neck when I ran and doubled in weight like a sponge whenever I sweat. It had grown ever longer and heavier in the years since her death, but I couldn't bear to cut it. She had grieved the loss of her hair so completely and had turned to me for comfort in those moments. How could I be so ungrateful as to think of this hair as a burden? It was the thing that made us look so alike. It was the symbol of her motherhood that I wore into the world. I owed her that much. Didn't I?

I grasped the hank of hair at the right side of my chin and set a pair of dull kitchen scissors to task. With eyes locked on my own reflection, I sawed through a quarter of the mass. The handful of hair I discarded unceremoniously in the tiny bathroom trash can was soon joined by the left side and my best effort at the back. I grinned manically as I chopped, feeling what wasn't there anymore. The weight of all that hair, no longer hanging around my neck—no longer pulling, clinging, tugging me back.

From what I could see in the mirror, I had done a decent job. The hair framing my face appeared even. When Lindy came home, she failed to conceal her horrified look. I had botched the thing. In an attempt to separate myself from the weight of my mother's hair, I had made a real mess.

Lindy's voice was firm but kind when she suggested that I go to a salon to get things evened out. I flatly refused. I could feel her gentle disapproval, but she saw that my scraggly hair was raw separation, an open wound—my independence.

Day 7: August 8, 2018
Nickel Creek → Indian Bar

THE HISSING AND ROLLING OF BOILING WATER ARE THE ONLY SOUNDS as Judah tiptoes around outside my tent. He notices me stirring as he packs and gives me a wink.

"Good morning, Sunshine!" I exclaim.

I spring into motion, setting my own water on the stove while I change clothes and pack up my sleep system and tent. Judah eyes my breakfast skeptically and I assure him that beet and kale chips in ramen is a true backpacker delicacy.

"You know, I never looked at the elevation profile of this trail before getting my permit," I tell Judah as we sling our packs round our shoulders and hit the trail, which turns immediately upward.

"Oh yeah?" He chuckles. "Bit off more than you can chew?"

"I don't think so. But I definitely wasn't mentally prepared for this amount of serious climbing. I guess I imagined that a trail *around* a mountain would not be a trail *up* a mountain. Silly me," I say. "I've heard the climb into Indian Bar is epic, although I can't imagine it being any worse than Emerald Ridge."

We pull over to study Judah's map, more as an excuse to take a break than to gain any new insight into the trail. The detailed map confirms we will continue gaining elevation for another three miles before a series of ups and downs into Indian Bar. We press on for another mile or so before stopping again.

Judah breaks out a gallon-size Ziploc bag stuffed with chocolate chip cookie bars which must weigh seven pounds. "Do you want one?"

I laugh out loud when I see it. "Did your wife make those?"

"Yeah, she always makes them for family trips and things." He grins.

I picture myself cheerfully making cookie bars for my husband to go on an awesome backpacking trip without me and writhe at the idea. There are a lot of things I wouldn't mind being left behind for, but backpacking? No way!

Sitting quietly nestled among the wildflowers on the side of the mountain, we munch cookie bars and listen to the buzzing of honeybees. I could live here forever, hiking the Wonderland Trail in rounds until the day I die on this hillside. How do people exist in so many ugly places while this heaven feels practically untouched?

I don't have much farther to go, but Judah has only begun a much longer day. He's hoping to make it all the way past Sunrise camp, around twenty miles to my 6.4, so we silently agree to keep moving and scurry back to the trail, trying not to trample the wildflowers.

For the next mile we are harangued by small black flies that pelt into our eyes, ears, nose, mouth, relentlessly buzzing and bumping into us. The sweat dripping from my forehead seems to call them from miles around, and our slow and steady pace is insufficient to escape. An elderly woman is gaining on us—every time I turn back to check, she is closer than the last.

We stop to douse ourselves in bug spray and the woman passes us. The flies don't seem at all bothered by our freshest layer of chemicals, and their numbers are not diminished as we continue. The woman speeds up the incline ahead and leaves us to deal with the pests.

Over the years, I have identified that there are two types of hikers—gliders and plodders. It doesn't seem to be dependent on age or fitness, but on how you carry your weight. With each step, I allow the entire weight of my body to transfer into one foot before moving the other. My feet take turns supporting my whole being. I am a plodder—I tromp, lumber, shuffle and trudge while others glide. As the woman glides out of sight ahead of us, and we plod along behind, I watch her feet touch lightly to the earth only to lift again instantly. Each footfall is followed immediately by a next step. There is grace and lightness in perpetual motion. The movement of a glider is efficient, which is why they arrive in camp with energy to spare, hours before the plodder drops their pack for the day with nothing left in the tank.

I wonder if it is possible for a plodder to become a glider. Maybe for a few moments at a time, maybe on a good day, maybe on a gentle downhill section of trail. But a true transformation? I can't imagine a day when I would start a new step before finishing that which came before. I would like to be the type of person who didn't feel the full weight of self in every step along the way; who could leave the pounding of head and heart out of the way of the toil of foot.

———

The next stretch of trail winds up through a meadow. It appears to be a gently rolling hillside, but the August sun beats down on our shoulders and the hills are anything but gentle. We make slow progress, perhaps a tenth of a mile at a time, stopping to pant and exchange weary looks. I wonder if Judah should go on without me. My pace is likely to prevent him from making his destination by nightfall.

Before I'm able to suggest it, a park ranger crests the hill in front of us, walking in our direction. Judah sees him too and turns back to me with an *oh, shit* look on his face. I shrug my shoulders almost imperceptibly.

"It's the middle of the day, that lady passed us on a day hike, why can't you be on a day hike?" I whisper urgently to Judah, hoping he can sell this convincingly to the ranger.

"Hey, how are you guys doing today?" the ranger calls to us as he approaches. He's almost bouncing up the trail, an offensive amount of pep in his step. I can't remember a time in my life I have ever moved along a hiking trail with such vigor, and I'm instantly peeved.

"Amazing! It's a perfect day." My heart races.

I'm not doing anything wrong; I have no responsibility for the actions of strangers on the trail.

"It is!" the ranger agrees. He is young and pimply-faced, with red hair and a uniform which hangs loosely on his gangly frame. "Can I see your permits?"

"Yup." I produce my permit and hand it over. I try not to look at Judah.

"This permit is for one," the ranger says.

"Yeah, that's mine," I say, "we just met."

I'm innocent! I was minding my own business when this guy showed up and started walking behind me.

"And your permit?" He hands mine back to me as he rounds on Judah.

"Oh, I'm on a day hike." Judah smiles uneasily.

I struggle to keep my face arranged in a know-nothing bystander sort of expression.

"Seems like you're carrying an awful lot of gear for a day hike." The ranger raises an eyebrow and the sweat on Judah's face makes him look as guilty as he is.

"I'm in training," he explains, "so, I carry the pack everywhere."

"I see." The ranger looks unsure of his authority here. He is, of course, the one with the badge, but he's also addressing a man twice his size and ten years his senior, and we're miles from the enforcement of societal roles and potential backup. It's basically the Wild Wild West out here. "Well, in case you were thinking about trying to camp without a permit, you should know there will be rangers patrolling throughout the night, and they *will* catch you."

"Oh no no, I'm getting out at Sunrise today. I have somebody picking me up there," Judah assures the ranger.

"Sunrise is pretty far." The ranger checks his watch. "It's already after one o'clock, you think you're going to make it?"

The tension is unbelievable and it's impossible to tell who is more intimidated by the other. Judah obviously knows he's in the wrong and the risk to his job if he gets caught must be real. The young ranger is clearly struggling to exert his authority in the situation. Perhaps this is his first brush with lawlessness on the trail.

"Well, so you know, the permitting rules are in place to protect the trail and reduce the footprint of hikers by keeping camping to designated areas. It's important because a lot of the area around the trail is fragile and easily disturbed." He trails off a bit at the end of his speech.

Nice job dude, keep it real, remind us why we're out here in the first place. Don't lose sight of the nature. This isn't a power struggle, it's about principles.

I know he's right and I feel a pang of guilt for befriending a rule-breaker. I believe in the National Park system and the rules they enforce. The ranger lets Judah off the hook with one last warning glance, and we go on our way. Judah shoots me a did-I-just-dodge-a-bullet look, and we breathe a collective sigh of relief.

"That dude knew I was full of shit," Judah blurts out as soon as he thinks we're out of earshot. I cringe and look back, half expecting the ranger to turn around. He doesn't.

"Well, you kind of are," I needle him, and the gravity of the moment dissipates.

"I should probably get a move on, if Sunrise is gonna be my story." He seems reluctant to leave me.

"Well good luck on your trip. I hope the rangers don't give you too hard of a time. And don't trample any delicate flora." We give each other a goofy high five and he accelerates away from me, making the pace we've been keeping look like a joke. He'd been plodding along just to hang out with me.

Gliders don't pretend to be plodders!

My solitude sinks in within a few minutes of his leaving. It's so rare to find someone who fits comfortably into my bubble, who walks right and talks right and doesn't set off my idiosyncratic annoyance bells. The trail is quiet, and for the first time, the inside of my head is equally tranquil. My overactive mind has played enough and is content to fall into a dreamy state as I cruise down the last stretch into Indian Bar.

The trail meanders through lush meadows sprinkled with

wildflowers of every color. The buzzing of bees in the flowers is an almost imperceptible hum. When I stop hiking and still my mind and trekking poles it grows a bit louder, as if the bees are proudly singing out for me. I pause in the middle of the trail and close my eyes, listening to the wind as it passes through the grass and feeling each lazy current and energetic gust as it acts upon my being.

I arrive at Indian Bar Campground less than an hour after Judah and I separate, but I'm certain he has long since gone. Indian Bar has been hyped as the most spectacular campsite on the trail and its beauty takes my breath away. A cozy stone cottage is nestled in a sprawling green valley between several prominent peaks, two glacial rivers converging on its front lawn.

The structure is reserved for the "group" party and could easily sleep twelve. The individual campsites set atop a small hill on the edge of the valley offer an idyllic view of the cottage and its inhabitants. I set up camp and skip down to have a look around. Five hikers in their twenties are setting up tents around the shelter when I walk up. They don't seem to notice me approaching through their jokes and the clacking of tent poles.

"Hey guys! I just wanted to check out the shelter, I heard this is the primo spot." I enter their space with open arms.

"K," says the only person who acknowledges my existence.

I shove my hands into my pockets and peek inside the shelter. Stone bunks and a dirt floor. Not much to see here. I look around for a trail log, the likes of which I haven't seen since Golden Lakes but find none.

"Uh, thanks," I offer as I slink away. The group continues to thoroughly ignore me.

I head down to the river with stuff sack full of socks and underwear. I test the temperature of the water with my hands—it's cold and moving swiftly. The area is shallow, safe enough to sit on a rock at the edge of the river with my legs dangling in while I scrub. Soon, my socks and spare underwear are arranged on the rocks around me. After a moment's debate I remove my hiking pants. They're eight days dirty and have the oil from a jar of almond butter spilled right on the front—surely a bear would be able to smell that.

Sitting in my underwear on the side of the river, I'm joined by a woman with her laundry, and we wash together. She is my campsite neighbor on the hill above and she's come down to soak her swollen knees in the cold water. As our clothes dry on the river's edge she sits fully in the water, her legs and hips completely submerged. I had no intentions to indulge the river so thoroughly but there is camaraderie to be had, and we suffer the prickling cold together for some time.

The conversation flows easily. She's probably twice my age and a dentist, on a backpacking trip with her brother and their friend. We have nothing in common besides a love of hiking and delight in this experience. After these topics wear themselves out, we talk about life and the struggles of young people in our current economy. Her children are dealing with a lot of the same challenges I had faced in Denver—low wages with unreasonable expectations, high rents, and inadequate benefits.

I tell her about living in my van and traveling the country alone. It's usually easy to discern a level of approval or disapproval at these statements, but she's difficult to read. She asks valid questions such as "Do you have health insurance?" rather than silly ones, like "Where do you go to the bathroom?" I'm grateful to her for making my acquaintance after being rejected by the group at the shelter. She asks me to join her party later for dinner.

There's a certain loneliness in meeting new people every day, sharing the cliff notes version of myself a hundred times and hearing the stories of a hundred strangers. I don't pretend to think this woman knows me now. I don't know her either. Perhaps we have learned or grown from this interaction, but it's just that—a single interaction.

Love comes with knowledge, and that's why there is no deeper love than that of a mother. She knows things nobody else ever will. She sees things even your best friend doesn't, loves parts of you even your lover can't touch. No person I meet now will know me in my entirety. They can look at pictures and hear stories, but they will never feel the joy of my toothless grin or wrap their arms around my teenage tears. Even my father doesn't know what it was like to bring me into this world, to be joined with me before he ever saw my face. My mother knew me in ways I never even knew myself. She left this earth when I was someone else. In her death, I became unknown. The me who began inside of her has been lost to the me walking through these woods.

Who will ever know me now?

Chapter 8

DENVER WAS NEVER MEANT TO BE MY PERMANENT HOME—I HAD planned to give it one year. But when that year was up, I wasn't ready to leave. So, I stayed. I settled in. It wasn't long before the stable, career-focused lifestyle began to feel like an elephant on my chest.

My time in Yosemite and on the Appalachian Trail had offered me a small window into a fascinating counterculture. I wanted to find a way to travel more—a way to exist and sustain myself between backpacking trips and rock-climbing destinations. There was a growing cohort of "van-lifers" who lived in converted cargo vans, fitting a tiny home in the space of a 138" wheelbase. The lifestyle was embraced by dirt-bag climbers long ago in order to work full-time doing what they loved. In recent years it had become popular among young professionals who took their work on the road and lived a life of miniature luxury, visiting National Parks and sleeping under the stars.

I couldn't think of a better way to live, taking my home with me from place to place. The freedom of the road called to me and I ached to answer. In a familiar position, clocking in and toiling away at my computer day in and day out, I dreamed of a journey where the rules no longer applied. Vanlife was the Appalachian Trail all over again. I had built a sturdy life—a far better one than that which I had left behind in Arkansas—but the confines of my existence in Denver were becoming suffocating, and I longed to throw it all out the window.

———

My stomach clenched and writhed as I watched Tucker hand over a stack of bills. The van was cute, no doubt about it— but it wasn't the van I had dreamed of. It was small—a classic Volkswagen—white with a deep, burgundy heart painted on one side. We had come all the way to Spearfish, South Dakota to look at this van, so we'd have to have a pretty good reason *not* to buy it at this point. And there was nothing wrong with this van—except for everything it represented. I couldn't even drive the thing; it was a stick shift. This was the van Tucker wanted. It was exactly what he had dreamed up over the last two months.

When I had told him about my plan to jump in a van and run away, explore the country and sleep under the stars, it all sounded too romantic. But he didn't understand that in my dream I was solo, riding off into sunsets without a care in the world. In my dream, every day started with asking myself, "Christine, what do you want to eat today?" And "Christine, what do you want to see today?"

He had commandeered my aspirations in a few short months, and suddenly my dream was *our* dream. He waxed poetic about the places we would go, the things we would see and how we would share everything, including a sixty-square-foot living space. He started shopping for vans and researching layouts for our bed and tiny kitchen. Tucker fired off onslaughts of Craigslist ads to my work email.

Ooh look at this one! And *What a great deal!*

As I tried to wrap my mind around the idea of sharing my dream, it became painfully apparent he was the last person I would want to do it with, but I was on a runaway train.

Tucker was jealous and whiny, making my life his own, becoming obsessed with my hobbies and never seeming to have anything going on if I wasn't there. Somehow, it seemed easier to go along with his scheming and hope things would figure themselves out in the end than to try to abort this mission. Besides, maybe it would be nice to have a partner. He could build things and fix things—skills I didn't possess.

The day he suggested we apply for a loan, my mother's voice rang in my ears. Her warnings about financial independence saturated my brain space. I knew, even in her absence, that this financial misstep was forewarned and inexcusable. In the moment, it felt strangely unavoidable—a mistake that needed to be made for the sake of deductive reasoning. How could I be sure this was something I was meant to do alone? How could I be sure this risk wasn't worth taking? I battled with the dichotomy of being an enlightened modern woman: stick to the script, get married, buy a house, raise a family—also be independent, take care of yourself, be guarded and untrusting.

Lindy and Laura had asked what I was thinking. Whatever I told them must have seemed convincing to me, although I can't quite remember what it was. It was obviously a crazy thing to do, but I'd come this far.

I maintained my composure as we had gathered around the dining room table to sign the title document. The tears didn't fall until we pulled out of the driveway—Tucker in the new van and me following in his little SUV. Our breakup started that day and lasted for weeks. Everything he said got under my skin, his voice became abrasive, and the van was the centerpiece of dozens of fights. We argued about when to buy new tires and how to pay for work on the starter. I wanted to paint it purple, he didn't want to drive a purple van. I had thought that living in a van would be all about what I wanted, and it began to feel like he had taken that from me while simultaneously dragging me into it.

I told him I wanted out. He resisted. He made me feel like the bad guy. He cried and played a convincing victim, while making menacing threats to ruin me with our loan. He told me I was a sociopath who didn't care about anyone while reminding me that he knew where I lived. Finally, he agreed to pay off the loan and switch the van into his name. It was the clean break I had been begging for, but he continued to call, and I never felt completely safe. The thing I thought would bring me freedom became my undoing. Eventually, I fled to Arizona, abandoning my life and my condo for the fresh air and expansive space of the desert. Running felt natural by now, and this time I had a concrete reason for it.

———

My eyes had been opened to a desire to share my life, a desire I had squashed and hidden long ago. I had vowed not to end up like my mother. She never truly had her own life after she met my father. She went where he went, following his career across the country and around the world. Her happiness was their partnership, and I truly believed she was happy. I had wished for a long time that I would find that type of happiness. At a certain point, I realized I would have to make myself happy.

I had tried to drown the desire for human connection with alcohol. I had tried serial casual dating and sex. I had pursued perpetually unavailable men and prided myself on my ability to refrain from attachments. It wasn't until I left Denver that I realized I wasn't as independent as I thought. Through my crazed yearning to avoid romantic commitment, I had built a family. Lindy, Laura and Andrew were my people. I didn't recognize what I had left behind until I'd been in Arizona for a couple months.

Between twelve-hour workdays and hour-long commutes, I hardly had time to notice I was lonely. I texted Lindy to tell her about the cute guy I'd met and my trip to Grand Canyon. When she told me she was going back to Tennessee to visit her parents, I worried about her. She and her mom struggled to understand each other. When we lived together in Denver, we often talked about our rebellions and our mothers' disapproval. She had a difficult relationship with her mother—one that made me truly appreciative for the one I'd had with mine.

I was standing in the office I shared with the store manager when I read her message and promptly sank into the rolling computer chair. My head spun at the words: *my mom killed herself this morning, about 6 hours ago.* I couldn't believe it. Of course, Lindy's mom had been threatening suicide for decades. It was something we had talked about at length. Now she had actually done it. Why now?

I racked my brain for some way to help, something I could do to take a little bit of the pain from my friend. But there was nothing to be done, and I was 1,750 miles away. I was impotent, useless. I fumbled through the rest of the day in a haze.

My mom's birthday was only four days away—that felt significant somehow. I thought of how afraid she had been to die, how she had told me she wasn't ready. She had cried when she'd asked me to sew names onto the cross-stitched stockings she had stored in the attic if I ever got married or had children. It broke her heart to think she wouldn't know who I called family in the future, but she wanted them to know she loved them.

I wondered how different it must feel to lose your mother because she was ready to go. She wanted to leave. I couldn't imagine the pain. I wanted to be there for Lindy, but our losses were so different. Over the next few days, I found excuses to work in the back room and avoid customers and coworkers whenever I could. I cried into cases of organic cereal and non-GMO crackers as I scanned them into inventory.

Lindy and I were together in our aloneness. I could feel her grief from across the country.

————

In the following months, I struggled to settle into my new home. I missed spending the evenings with Lindy after work, sharing stories about our days and comparing notes on the men in our lives. I tried to date, but with my hectic schedule and progressive feelings of isolation, I couldn't seem to make anything stick.

I wanted a partner who was as fierce and independent as I was. Someone with their own dreams and aspirations, someone filled with joy and wonder and a desire to experience everything. The problem with men who burn with the fire of exploration is that they never stick around. I fell in love and fell in love again. The first in a new line of men found me licking my wounds in Arizona and encouraged me that this failure didn't have to mean the end of vanlife dreams.

We were inseparable for weeks. He went with me to find a new van—looking under hoods and kicking tires on a weekend trip to Las Vegas. When I handed over the cash for her purchase, she was undoubtedly mine. She was nothing special but exactly how I imagined: a 2003 Dodge Ram Van, black and homely, only fifteen years old but in the style of a much earlier decade. I named her Celeste in honor of the celestial bodies, with whom I hoped to become better acquainted during my life on the road.

He never suggested this journey would become ours, and after helping me rip out the seats and carpet and install a modest plywood floor, we saw each other for the last time before the bed was even built.

Day 8: August 9, 2018
Indian Barr → Summerland

My muscles complain as I stretch and roll over in my sleeping bag. The heat of the direct sunlight turns my tent into an oven, and I won't be able to keep these wool layers on for long. Only 4.5 miles to Summerland, a short day, so I take my time changing into my freshly washed hiking pants and packing up my gear.

With my loaded pack slung over one shoulder, I search for a boulder comfortable enough to cook and eat breakfast on, set up my stove and settle in. I share my morning with the river, dipping my feet into the icy water and studying the way it arranges itself to rush over and between the rocks, while simultaneously organizing and shaping them to suit itself.

"How do you know which rock you should navigate around, and which will move for you?" I ask. "How do you decide whether energy is better spent in the reshaping of a particular stone, softening its edges, smoothing its surface or whether you would be better off pushing the stone along, helping it to find a better place to rest?"

I close my eyes and listen as the river speaks, its voice a cacophony of whooshing and splashing. These are life's biggest questions, and perhaps a river doesn't have the answer any more than I do. Perhaps it acts upon all stones with the same force and allows them to choose—an elegant solution in its simplicity but perhaps graceless in practice.

Stones that have broken free from the place where they once lay tumble along, bumping and crashing into their fellows, sometimes threatening to break with the force. They search for a pleasant-looking spot where they might settle in. Other rocks are nestled, wedged together to prevent each other from shifting, leaving no room for those in motion. It's impossible to slow down enough to test out a potential home before being swept further downstream and away. Each rolling stone is on its own journey. The water pushes them this way and that. Their paths intersect at random before diverging again. I wonder if they're destined to roll away forever. Or perhaps somewhere at the end of the river is a pile of lonely stones brought together by nothing more than the fact they had nowhere else to go.

I'm entangled in my thoughts when I rise from the river and find the trail again. As I amble out of the valley, I turn back for one more look at the picturesque cottage and marvel at the splendor tucked into this one tiny dot on the map. The whooshing of the river echoes in my mind long after it has left my ears.

———

Rolling hills and grassy meadows give way to boulder fields and long slopes of loose scree throughout the day. With no canopy above to protect me from its unforgiving rays, the sun beats down and penetrates my skin. My shoulders are hot to the touch. A small stream crosses the trail, offering a place to soak my bare feet and filter cool water to drink. I dip my bright yellow bandanna and tie it around my neck like a kerchief, beholding the very Boy Scout nature of the thing. I remember the sunscreen left behind in Longmire—so much for always being prepared.

Beads of water drip down my back as I walk on, tickling and cooling beneath my heavy sweat-soaked pack. I spot a snow patch in the distance with a clear trail cut through it. With the record high August temperatures and dangerous river swelling, I had assumed I wouldn't be crossing any snow fields. The snow melting much higher on the mountain should have left no traces at only 6,000 ft elevation. Yet here I am, staring down two hundred feet of snow and ice, crunchy and slick from the temperature fluctuations and packed down by hundreds of footsteps.

A group of hikers is stepping onto the snow from the opposite direction. From a distance, I can see they aren't using trekking poles but are holding their arms out for balance and leaving a substantial following distance to avoid a domino effect if someone falls. They wait for their last member, a particularly large and ungainly man, to make his way back onto dry rock as I approach.

Witnessing their clumsy traverse hasn't given me confidence in the stability of the shallow trench cut into the snow. It gleams in the midday sun, suggesting a slippery and treacherous crossing. I cautiously place one foot into the path and slide it back and forth, testing out the traction on my trail runners. These shoes aren't made for snow but seem to be capable. My nerves are immediately calm, and I cross efficiently, my trekking poles poking deep holes on each side of the route.

The bright white of the snow leaves sparkles in my vision

for several minutes after my return to rock hopping. As my surroundings come back into focus, movement off the trail catches my attention. I stop to watch as a family of ptarmigans navigate over the boulders. The mother has a white and brown speckled pattern with immaculate feathers. The eight chicks lined up behind her resemble little fur poufs with tiny stick legs popping out the bottom. The chicks run to keep up, their little legs scrambling to stay under their little round bodies. It's ridiculously adorable. One chick loses its legs completely and rolls over, sliding into the crack between two rocks. It cheeps urgently as it struggles to regain its feet, and the others chirp back with encouragement. It rights itself and quickly joins its brothers and sisters on their journey.

The chicks spend their youth trailing behind their mother, learning where to find food and shelter and how to navigate the boulder fields they call home. One day they'll be ready to find a mate and eventually traverse the same obstacles with a train of their own little chicks following behind. It's the circle of life, as inevitable and uncomplicated as the changing of the seasons. These chicks don't consider striking out on their own, they don't wonder if their mother is the model after which they want to live. They do not resist becoming like her for fear their lives could be better.

Over the next ridge lies another snow field, much shorter but far more precarious than the first. A 100-foot section of the trail has long since been washed out, and the path through it hugs the inside of a sheer drop off. The narrow thoroughfare has been flattened by foot traffic but not intentionally shaped in any meaningful way. About thirty feet of this section is covered with snow, and the path happens to wander directly below a car-sized boulder which has likely been perched just so for at least a decade, though it appears as if it could let go at any second.

I scan the trail to see if any hikers are coming and might see or hear me if I meet my demise, but alas, I'm all alone. With one deep steadying breath, I step onto the icy snow. My breathing is sharp and ragged as I sneak under the boulder.

Don't panic, just breathe, everything is fine. Hundreds of people have walked here, under this boulder, and they are all probably fine. Don't. Panic.

On the other side, my heart races. High with the intensity of it all, I let out a guttural exclamation. I think again of the dangers of backpacking and how misunderstood they are. My father probably never imagined me being crushed by a precarious boulder.

An aquamarine lake lies at the bottom of the rocky slope ahead of me. I've never seen water that color in nature, and it sparkles up at me like a thousand diamonds. The path from here to there squiggles down over the rocks and is littered with hikers. There are twenty people out here, when five minutes ago I thought I was in total solitude. There must be parking at Summerland.

The campsite must be overrun with tourists, which would explain the recent reports of bear activity in the Summerland area. I power through the last half mile down to the lake as if hypnotized by its glimmering surface. Dropping my pack on the rocky banks and thoroughly ignoring the day hikers on the edge of the lake, I leave a trail of clothing as I walk into the water. Even close up, the dazzling blue-green is surreal: clear enough to see my feet sinking into the silty bottom beneath and bright enough that the reflected sunlight seems to be originating from the lake itself. The snow ringing the north edge of the lake gleams magnanimously, having given life to this lovely creation, but not at all concerned with taking credit.

In an instant, I register the frigid temperature of the water and the sludgy ground beneath it before closing my eyes and plunging into its depths. Gasping as I break the surface, I desperately scramble back to my feet. Shivering, I lay down on a large flat rock to dry off. Between the warm rock on my back and the sun beaming down, the cold begins to subside.

———

Summerland is less than a mile beyond the unnamed lake, and even after a luxurious break, I make it to camp long before dinner time. An adorable stone cottage, smaller than the one at Indian Bar, is occupied by a group of fast-talking, thickly-accented New Yorkers. I stop to say hello, and they are overly friendly—asking dozens of questions about the Wonderland Trail, in stark contrast with the standoffish group I met yesterday. They insist on giving me some of their snacks. Which I half-heartedly pretend to turn down, before stuffing them in my face. A chubby, precocious chipmunk darts in and out of the group trying to nab some for himself.

"Hey, watch that little guy, I'm sure he is used to being fed," I say. "He might get bold with your dried mango."

One of the girls picks up the bag of dried mangoes and tucks them into her pack—the chipmunk looks dismayed but not defeated.

Just up the hill beyond, I explore the individual campsites and hang my food bag on the bear pole. After setting up my tent and changing into camp shoes, I head back down to the shelter. The day hikers have moved on and a young woman is setting up a tent on the wooden platform.

"Hi, I'm Christine, do you mind if I hang around with you for a while tonight?" I ask. "I've been alone all day!"

"Oh yeah, totally, I'm Annie, my partner Odessa went

down to jump in the river." Her smile is broad, her face open.

She tells me that they're both doctors in a small community on the Olympic Peninsula. She talks about being almost thirty and married and thinking about having children. I try to relate to anything she says but find it challenging at best. I was a busy business lady once, or twice. It always left me itching to run away, though she seems quite happy.

In the past week, I've been repeatedly asked about my aloneness—if I'm alone and why am I alone. Annie hasn't asked, but I feel compelled to explain myself anyway. I can't help but feel defensive when a bright, capable young woman has chosen the script and forgone the opportunity to live defiantly against expectation. My mind is clouded with judgement, even as I am beginning to realize that independence is about making choices for your own life. Those choices don't have to be in direct opposition to societal expectation to be independent. I ramble on about my nomadic life and the choices that led me here, hoping that perhaps by the end of my diatribe one of us will have a better understanding.

She is both kind and receptive, and the conversation remains friendly. Even so, I leave feeling bitter and filled with self-doubt. I excuse myself and head back to my tent, insides roiling. The sun is still shining, but I have a lot to think on and suddenly want to be alone in my aloneness again.

I settle onto my sleeping bag, using my pack as a back rest, and pull out my Wilderness Trip Planner Map to study the remainder of my trip. Tomorrow is ten or so miles to Sunrise Camp, with a stop at the White River Campground to pick up my second food cache. Then almost eleven miles to Mystic Camp the following day, around five miles to Carbon River the next day and eight miles back to Mowich

Lake on my final day. It's hard to believe my trip is already two thirds done—I think back to the first and second day when I questioned my decision to be out here at all, when I considered getting off at Longmire and forgetting about backpacking forever.

A scrambling noise and flash of dark fur grabs my attention. I look up in time to see a marmot hurtling through my campsite. Whoa! I have never seen a marmot move like that. Unzipping the sheer mesh side of my tent, I poke my head out to get a better look, but it's long gone. Shrugging, I zip my tent back up and continue looking at my map. Soon, I hear rustling and a series of loud thumps. Suddenly, two black bears barrel out of the trees from whence the marmot has come. My stomach leaps into my throat as they round on me.

Holy shit. Ohmygod. Stay calm, they are only black bears. The ranger said they have never attacked anyone before. Don't freak out. Freaking out will not help.

They've obviously been following the marmot, but undoubtedly my presence is more interesting. Within seconds they're flanking me, one on each side of my tiny backpacking tent. If I had the audacity to do so, I could reach out and pet them each on the head.

What do I do? They're not supposed to get this close. Should I yell at them? That doesn't seem safe, what if I scare them? What if they attack me? What do I do?

I make eye contact first with the bear on the right—his nostrils flare as he consumes my scent. I then look to the one on the left. Seconds stretch on like hours, the bears peering curiously into my face as I try to keep my breathing steady. Certainly, they can hear the deafening pounding of my heart.

What do I smell like to a bear? Can they smell the lake I

jumped in, the ramen I ate for breakfast, the almond butter oil I tried to scrub from the front of my hiking pants?

These are not full-grown bears—yearlings maybe. There must be a mother around here somewhere. My vulnerability in this position is undeniable; I can't stand up to make myself appear larger. Even if I could, I'm too afraid to move.

As suddenly as they came, the bears turn and scamper off, to pursue the marmot. Every muscle in my body is locked tight but my mind is frantic. I can't decide if it's safe to get out of my tent. Surely the bears will realize the marmot has taken advantage of their delay to make a thorough escape and return to investigate me further. A mother bear must be nearby, supervising their hunt and perhaps following along behind. Several ragged breaths rattle my body before I'm able to call out to my fellow campers.

"Hello?" My voice is hollow. I doubt it's loud enough for anyone to hear. No response. Nobody comes rushing into my campsite to see if I'm alive. So, these are the bears everyone's been talking about. The ones I should be afraid of. The reason women should be afraid to hike alone. That was by far the scariest thing that has ever happened to me in the great outdoors.

With trembling hands, I unzip the door of my tent and lurch to my feet. My knees quake as I stagger down to the stone shelter, deliberately avoiding breaking into a run, though the instinct is strong. As I approach, I call out to Annie and Odessa.

"Hey, if either of you are interested in seeing a bear, a couple of them went that way." The quiver is my voice is difficult to suppress as I point behind me.

"What?! You saw a bear?" Annie says. The envy on her face is satisfying, but she doesn't realize how closely I saw not one bear, but two.

"Two! They came right up to me." I nod. My heart is still racing, and my head swims as I recount the experience. Annie's eyes go all buggy and she offers space for me to camp in the shelter with them.

"I think I'll be okay up there, they've seen me now, so they know I'm there, so I should be fine tonight, I think." I heap on the false confidence.

A group of hikers runs up to the shelter, the leader grasping a fancy digital camera.

"Did you girls see the bears?" they ask excitedly.

"Yeah, I saw two cubs, over there." I point back.

"Oh, we saw a mom and a cub, down there." They indicate the opposite direction.

Oh no, we're surrounded.

"There must be four of them then," I say.

We all exchange excited looks—seeing a bear is a rite of passage in backpacking culture, and the others have had the safer and considerably less terrifying experience of snapping a photo of one from a distance. They show us a few pictures of the mom and third cub before skipping off to their campsites.

"I'm going to go ahead and stay up there for the night. I'm not far from that other group—I think I'll be okay. Black bears are more afraid of us than we are of them," I say, remembering the ranger's assurance that there had never been a bear incident in Mount Rainier.

Back at my tent, I stretch the rain fly over the mesh walls before entering. At least I won't be able to look them in the eyes while they decide whether to eat me next time. I crawl into my sleeping bag and close my eyes. A tree branch rustles.

Oh my god, a bear! No. It wasn't a bear. It's just a tree. It's fine.

My heart beats erratically. Nature is making nature sounds, and every single one could be a bear. How can anyone sleep like this?

Minutes pass before I admit defeat and head back down to the shelter where Annie and Odessa are getting settled in for the night. They welcome me into their space, and Annie even offers to help me carry my tent and gear down the hill.

I lay down in bed for the third time within the hour. Odessa is cowboy-camping with her bedroll laid out directly on the ground less than ten feet from my tent. She's obviously way more hardcore than me. Or maybe that kind of confidence comes with knowing you're not alone out here.

Chapter 9

THE OPEN ROAD HAD BEEN PAINTED IN MY MIND: STRAIGHT AND CURVY, surrounded by desert and mountains, following the coastline, clear blue skies and twinkling stars. I had visualized days spent basking in the glow of the natural world and forgetting about the life I had left behind. I longed to remember where my soul came from.

Everything was not so simple as that. I had friends and family I wanted to visit and a van with no bed in it. I craved a return to Denver, to the home I had left behind in my desperate escape. I drove straight there and parked my new van in Laura and Andrew's driveway. Their guest room was a home away from home during the days it took for me to piece together a couple of two-by-fours and a sheet of plywood to build a platform bed.

I knew at the outset I lacked the carpentry and electrical skills to set the van up myself. It quickly became apparent that I had underestimated the level of skill required for what seemed like basic tasks. Andrew looked on as I puzzled with the lengths of wood before helpfully suggesting I pick up some brackets at the hardware store. Laura and I squealed with girlish delight after I made my first cut with the circular saw.

The skills I had learned in my life didn't seem to be applicable anymore, though I had been led to believe they would facilitate my independence. I was well read and could write a persuasive argument. I could cook and sew on a button. I could balance my checkbook and run an entire retail operation. Somehow, I had been robbed of the kind of independence that comes from handy skills, and instead been bestowed the skills of a wage worker.

What would I do when the van broke down in the middle of nowhere? My parents had taught me to be cautious, to be afraid, to recognize danger. They didn't teach me the necessary skills for true self-reliance. They sent me from the nest with hopes that I wouldn't fly too far, hopes that I would avoid danger rather than manage it. They wanted me to play it safe; become boring and practical.

When I envisioned myself standing on the side of a highway in the desert, with a hundred miles of flat nothing stretching out in every direction and the heat waves of the engine blending into the heat haze of the desert, I couldn't quite picture myself with a wrench in my hand turning bolts and wiping sweat from my forehead. It was all too easy to imagine an unsavory driver of an eighteen-wheeler pulling up, rolling down the window, and offering some terrifying rendition of "Cash, Grass, or Ass?"

———

It was the first week of May, and stifling air whipped through the open windows as the blazing sun baked Celeste's black exterior. The upholstered driver's seat soaked up my sweat and I stacked my hair heavily on top of my head to keep it away from my neck and face. The hot asphalt slid beneath my wheels and the engine temperature gauge crept higher. I was on my way to see my dad, to show him my new home. When I had first sent him a photo of Celeste, he told me I was very funny. I was sure he'd be even more pleased if she left me stranded in the middle of Kansas. I pulled over to check for a leak.

Crouching beside the front driver's tire, I sighed at the unmistakable drip of green coolant on the sweltering asphalt. The smell of the hot engine filled my nostrils as I walked into the truck stop to pick up a jug of coolant. I would have to keep an eye on the gauge and stop to pour more coolant in if it got too high. I stashed the jug in the passenger floorboard and flipped the air conditioning to heat before merging back onto the highway. I could easily take Celeste into a shop when I got to Little Rock, but I couldn't stop here. I glanced nervously at the dash display.

A hundred miles later, the temperature began to rise again. I cursed the long open road and miles between dots of civilization. I searched for a mechanic as I approached Edson and Brewster, but nothing was open on a Sunday afternoon. Between Denver and Topeka, I-70 cuts through 541 miles of farmland sprinkled with convenience stores and small highway churches whose congregations were at that very moment driving home for Sunday lunch. Every small-town mechanic specialized in Dodge, Ford, and John Deere engines—and every one of them was closed for the day.

At a truck stop in Colby, Kansas I asked if the shop could take a look at a non-commercial vehicle for a desperate girl. The waiting room smelled strongly of oil and dirt. A big trucker looked up from a six-year-old issue of Car and Driver magazine, causing me to instantly regret my appearance. My black running shorts and neon yellow tank top clung to my body with sweat and my long legs suddenly felt inappropriately exposed under the direct blast of the air conditioning in the small room. The mechanic huffed and puffed when I told him my cooling system was leaking.

"What kind of vehicle?" he asked.

"It's a 2003 Dodge Ram Van, right there." I pointed at the van sitting innocently outside the window.

"We don't really do that here," he hedged.

"It's just, you're the only place open and I need to know if it's safe to keep driving. I need to get home today," I pleaded.

He sighed, "okay, let me take a look at it."

Twenty minutes later he came in to inform me the water pump was leaking pretty heavily, and they could replace it, but there were four trucks in line. It would be several hours before they could work on it. I weighed my options and decided sitting at this truck stop for most of the day was better than getting stranded on the side of the highway in the middle of Kansas. They ordered the part, and I settled in on the decrepit black pleather couch.

Minutes crawled by as I feigned interest in the singing competition on the waiting room TV. I flipped idly through a selection of magazines and wrote in my journal. The trucker eventually left, leaving me alone in the chilly room. Hours ticked by and the sun crossed the sky before the mechanic came back to inform me that they wouldn't be able to change the water pump after all. A specialty tool was required, and nobody in the shop had one. He assured me that they could do it the next day, but I couldn't wait. I asked him to top off my coolant and he sent me on my way with a water pump, new in box, for cost.

I was filled with fresh confidence as I crossed through Wichita and into Oklahoma without issue. After a quick stop just outside Oklahoma City, the temperature spiked, forcing me to pull off the interstate almost immediately. Hours later I found myself in the garage of a firefighter-slash-tow-truck-driver, who had kindly offered to work on my van rather than drop me in front of a shuttered auto shop.

I watched as he and his buddies chain smoked under the hood of my Celeste. It took no less than six hours for them to replace the water pump, which is conveniently located just behind and underneath every other part of the engine. Around midnight, I finally rolled out of town and about an hour later I stopped to sleep in the parking lot of an Indian Casino. Gratitude and surprise at the kindness of strangers filled me. It couldn't override a fear that dictated I get far enough out of town that they couldn't find me.

———

After making a circle through Arkansas, Louisiana, and Texas, catching up with family and old friends, I was free to head west to figure out what this vision was about. I was instantly filled with doubt. I couldn't quite pin down what exactly I was trying to accomplish. I didn't know where I was going or who or what I was hoping would be there waiting for me.

I found myself pointed back toward the desert, toward the comfort and mystery it held. I had only lived in Arizona for four months, most of it working long hours and commuting. There was so much still to do. Plus, Bureau of Land Management and Forest Service land makes up about 32% of the state. This makes it especially conducive to nomadic living, as most of that land is available for free and easy camping. However, within days of my arrival the state shut the gates on many public areas due to fire danger, and I was forced to move on.

When I shoved off from Arizona in mid-May, I had nowhere known left to go. I studied a map and decided my first landing spot would be Las Vegas. It was only a five-hour drive, which would leave me plenty of time to get comfortable and search for a good camping spot before sunset. I was still nervous about pulling up to a congregation of vehicle dwellers and making myself known. There are all sorts of people who camp in Walmart parking lots and on BLM land, so you never know what you're getting into.

My old climbing gym in Colorado had a parking lot full of converted vans. I guessed that Las Vegas must be similar, maybe I could make a friend. I chose a gym at random from the list in the Vegas area and pulled up several hours later to the deserted parking lot of a warehouse complex. It was the middle of the day, but I was still surprised by how empty it was. Maybe the vans parked in the back. As I rounded the building, one lonely white van was parked with a small trailer. The trailer had a big decal on the side, one I'd seen before.

I knew this person, except I didn't. We had never met, but I knew exactly who was standing inside that trailer, wearing big, noise-canceling headphones and safety glasses, his shoulder length hair tied up in a ponytail. I had heard about him—from his best friend—who also happened to be a good friend of mine. He looked up when I pulled in next to his van and turned off the loud machine he was working on. I jumped down from the driver's seat to introduce myself. The road provides.

"Hey, are you Isaac?" I asked.

He searched my face for something familiar.

"We haven't met. You know Joey? He told me about you," I said.

I took stock of his dirty, sweat-smeared face. The few silver hairs mixed in with his light brown. He was surprisingly handsome.

"Oh, he told you I was going to be here?" His voice was a combination of a soft southern accent and a stoked climber from Colorado.

"No. Actually, he told me about you and your business, months ago. I was stopping through here to see if I could find out where the cool van people were hanging out, and I saw you." We both smiled.

I was going to spend the evening alone, but instead I found an unexpected friend. We spent the evening walking the strip and eating the "World's Best Gyros." So much for my first night alone in the unknown. Isaac seemed just as hungry for companionship as I was.

"Why are you doing this? The van thing?" he asked over dinner.

"Isn't it the dream? I can go wherever I want, do whatever I want." I smiled.

"Yeah, but why live in a van? I'm kind of over it to be honest." He frowned.

"Oh…" I wasn't sure what to say to that.

"Like, aren't you lonely? Don't you miss people?" he asked.

"Sure. But I'm a strong independent woman. I want to see the world," I said.

"What good is seeing the world if you're alone all the time?"

"I guess I'm not alone all the time. I'm here with you now." I smiled hopefully.

I couldn't believe he was so disenchanted with the life I'd been dreaming of. Fear gripped me as I considered that I had been wrong about my dream. Maybe it wasn't all it was cracked up to be.

I thought of Lindy and Laura, of my life back in Denver. I missed our game nights and girls' nights—Laura's backyard with the fire pit and the gluten free s'mores. It was the only place that felt like home to me anymore. It had been a long time since my stomach hurt from laughter. I looked into Isaac's sorrowful eyes and wondered who he was missing.

Day 9: August 10, 2018
Summerland → Sunrise Camp

I WAKE WITH THE SUN FOR THE FIRST TIME AFTER DEEP, UNINTERRUPTED sleep. It must be around five o'clock. Annie and Odessa are quiet. I hesitate to jump from my tent too quickly—a bear could be moseying around in the dawn light. However, I'd like to get a move on my day. Some alone time on the trail with my feet and my thoughts will be nice after such an eventful evening. The nylon roof over my head filters the morning sun like a lampshade but hides the beautiful color display. I whip open the side door and the outer rainfly, revealing a sky painted with pinks and oranges fading fast as the sun prepares to make its debut.

Curled in my sleeping bag, I watch the sunrise until the sky is white and blue and completely lacking the rainbow spectacle of rising light. I try to pack up silently but fail to sneak out unnoticed. Odessa and Annie bid me goodbye as I walk out of camp.

I float down the first four miles of trail. The steady, forgiving descent is welcome to my legs and mind. The meadows surrounding Summerland transition smoothly into wooded glades with shafts of sunlight streaming through the canopy. There is serenity in the gentle rustling of leaves, and the clean, wet smell of the adjacent Fryingpan Creek permeates the air. With every inhale the love of the forest fills my body, and with every exhale I release a little bit of my anxiety.

In the valley between Summerland and the White River Campground, I hear rumors from day hikers about a bridge out farther down the trail. The White River has risen above the level of the bridge, and crossing is increasingly dangerous. An alternate route follows a mile or so of road walking in place of the same amount of trail.

If I go around and the river isn't even that high, I'll miss a piece of the trail. Some thru-hikers would discredit their whole hike if they had to skip a mile of trail. That type of completionist attitude has always rubbed me the wrong way though, and I refuse to put myself in danger over something so silly.

I arrive at a fork in the road—the alternate route towards the White River trailhead is on the right and the Wonderland Trail continues on the left. A laminated warning sign is taped sloppily to the signpost. The warning reads: "Due to high heat, glacial rivers are running very high. If a bridge looks unsafe to cross, use extreme caution in finding an alternate route." It specifically suggests taking the road here and avoiding the White River Bridge. After a lengthy deliberation, I direct my feet to the Wonderland Trail.

If I get to the river and it's in bad shape, I can always turn back.

I take three steps before stopping and wheeling around. I shouldn't risk it. I march purposefully back to the fork and proceed out to the trailhead. I know myself, and I know that if faced with backtracking a mile, I am just as likely to do something marginally dangerous as turn back. Sometimes laziness trumps fear, and I should avoid putting myself in the position to make that decision.

I pound the pavement for a solid twenty minutes, following the signs to the White River Campground. Only a few cars pass as I walk. Entering the campground is like stepping into another world. It's only been four days since Longmire, but time away from civilization has a way of stretching on. The mind tends to adjust to a certain way of thinking in the woods. Walking among the RV mansions and two-room tents, I scoff at the luxury.

My food cache awaits behind the Ranger Station, and I pluck a sugary chocolatey granola bar from the hiker box. At a picnic table next to the trailhead parking lot, I jam the new food into my stuff sack. My cook pot and titanium spork are crusted with the remnants of oats and ramen, so I scrub them in the bathroom sink. A woman comes into the restroom while I'm washing my face and gives me a suspicious look. I wonder what seems off-key about washing my face in a campground bathroom.

Piled next to a trash can outside is a collection of containers which I can only assume were originally food caches. I leave mine there and head right back to the trail. I see no reason to hang around in White River, there's nothing here but the campsite. Next stop—Sunrise.

The ascent out of the White River Campground passes quickly, although it's no less challenging than many others I have tackled on the trail. I've grown accustomed to powering up and down steep hills, and my fully loaded pack doesn't seem to weigh on my shoulders as intensely as it did eight days ago.

It's still early enough when I approach Sunrise that day hikers are heading in the opposite direction. I exchange pleasantries over and over again, being told repeatedly that I'm getting close. One of my favorite-least-favorite parts of hiking culture is the overwhelming desire of other hikers to tell me how far I am from "the thing." Most of these interactions grate on me in a way I find difficult to describe, but it goes something like this:

"Hey, you're almost there!" says some well-meaning, but clueless, jackanape.

"Great, thanks!" I reply, while thinking loudly: *How do you even know where I'm going? Do I look like I need encouragement or something? Am I struggling that much? YOU'RE almost there! YOUR MOM is almost there!*

Literally minutes later, I'm still rolling my eyes. I don't mean to be a Negative Nancy, but whatever happened to a nice asinine comment on the weather, or a simple hello and move along?

I reach another fork in the road—Sunrise Camp to the left and the Sunrise Visitor's Center, restaurant and tourist area to the right. It turns out the trail does not pass directly through the tourist area. I debate walking into Sunrise with my pack on to avoid backtracking versus heading to camp and setting up before going in. Having to make a second decision in one day is more than I had bargained for. Due to the overly scheduled nature of this thru-hike, I had counted on a reprieve from decision fatigue. But here I am.

Left or right? Left? Right?

As I tromp toward camp, I am proud that at the end of a long day of hiking, I choose to walk a little further. I remember days on the Appalachian Trail when I couldn't be convinced to walk any distance that wasn't necessary or required.

Go see a sweet fire tower 0.6 miles off trail? No thank you!

I pitch my tent as far away from a loud group of teenage boys as I can manage. It's a perfect sixty degrees, and the trail back to Sunrise is flat and dusty. In my sandals and fleece jacket, I walk back to the tourist area. I grin at the prospect of a fresh meal and a new book, cheerfully greeting day hikers the whole way in.

In Sunrise, the Visitor's Center stands across the parking lot from the gift shop. I enter the Visitor's Center to see if they keep a log of animal sightings, assuming they would want to know about my bear encounter. As I scan the last few pages of the logbook, I find only a couple of bear reports, but a load of marmots and pikas have been spotted. I wouldn't have even thought to report a marmot sighting, in barely more than a week I've seen at least a dozen.

The ranger who handed the notebook over asks me about my sighting, and by the time I've finished telling the story, the other two rangers at the desk are listening in. Some park guests filtering through don't even attempt to disguise the looks of horror on their faces.

"Where did that happen? Here!?" one woman demands.

"Oh no, like ten miles from here, at Summerland campsite, way out in the woods," I say.

"But they came right up to you?" She's incredulous.

"Well they didn't realize I was there until it was too late. They probably wouldn't have come so close if they had known. They didn't seem threatening," I say with epic nonchalance. It's much easier to act cool about the whole thing now that I'm safe in the Visitor's Center.

I make a quick exit from the conversation and head over to the cafeteria-style restaurant across the parking lot. The place is bustling with families eating lunch, but luckily a group gets up to leave as I'm handed my tray. Alone in a sea of strangers, I eat a mediocre veggie burger. The commotion of the dining room is overly intense after days of near silence on the trail.

On the opposite side of a row of bookshelves filled with trinkets and souvenirs sits the gift shop. I peruse the candy and snacks section to find a ridiculously priced dark chocolate bar. The book selection is nothing short of disappointing. The small shelf is laden with hiking and climbing guidebooks—more variety than I could imagine would exist for a single mountain. And that's it. Other than guidebooks, there is one sad lonely memoir on the top shelf. It's a modest volume, olive green with a painting of Mt. Rainier on the front. It screams "I'm a book!" and not much more than that. I read the back and am vaguely interested. The author was a climbing ranger on Mt. Rainier for a few seasons, battling the challenges of safety and customer service and the dynamics of being a young woman in a male-dominated field.

Standing in line to pay for the chocolate and the book, I gaze off into space to avoid being sucked into the energy of the room. As the queue moves slowly forward, I make eye contact with one of the cashiers and am sure I recognize her. But I can't place her.

"Christine?" she says, surprised.

Oh no! She knows my name. What is her name?

"Julie!" I read off her name tag.

Julie and I both lived in Yosemite National Park during the winter of 2014. We've met before but she was better friends with Lindy than with me.

"What are you doing here?" she asks.

"I'm on my ninth day on the Wonderland Trail," I say.

"NO WAY! So cool!" Her eyes light up.

She rings up my items, and I pay.

"Well, it was good to see you!" I tell her lamely and walk out of the shop, marveling at the coincidence.

As I step onto the deck of the shop, she opens the door behind me.

"Hey, do you want a shower or something?" she offers.

My gut instinct when offered what seems like ridiculous hospitality is to decline, as I rarely choose to indebt myself to the kindness of others.

"Yeah, definitely!" I say. I've been working on this, because as it turns out, allowing others to show you kindness is as important as showing kindness to others. Spreading joy is not a one-way mission.

"Here, let me show you around. You can shower and then I'll be on my lunch break in, like, thirty minutes." Julie is psyched to pay it forward in the park community, and it feels befitting to share this experience with a familiar face.

The water runs brown around my ankles as I pull my fingers through squeaky-clean hair. Standing under the steaming spray far longer than is truly necessary, I reflect on the luck of the situation. This is the kind of trail magic I only dreamed of on the Appalachian Trail.

In the employee community room, I settle onto a shabby sofa with sagging threadbare cushions. The employee housing resembles a dorm, with doors lining the main hall; each decorated with the employee's name, some standing open in communal welcoming. The building could best be described as run-down, with a messy, homey feeling about it. I immediately imagine myself living here. It's become a habit over the years to picture myself happily existing in almost any setting. The fantasy of making a new home everywhere

I go is quite appealing.

Julie comes to fetch me, and we hang out in the employee break room while she eats lunch. I tell her about my hike, and she tells me about some of the other trails in the park. She asks about Lindy, and I feel the niggling guilt of my absence. I tell her Lindy's okay, but I don't know the truth of that statement. I've hardly been with Lindy since her mother's passing and we haven't talked about it much. She seems to be holding herself together, but it's difficult to know at such a distance.

I don't let my heavy heart displace my gratitude for Julie. As a solo wanderer, I've spent time in many transient communities. Between living in a National Park and hiking a section of the Appalachian Trail, I've made friends all over the country. There is an interconnectedness in these communities that goes beyond my personal relationships. We share something profound, a passion and a searching that is universally understood. Even when I'm feeling lost and alone, I'm never as far from friends as I think I am.

———

Dust from the trail collects on my wet sandals as I depart the visitors' area of Sunrise. I smile affectionately at my dirty little freshly washed toes. As I again reach the intersection with the Wonderland Trail, two women meet me at the sign. They are bedecked with large packs and trekking poles and it escapes my mind that I am not.

"Hey! Are you ladies thru-hiking the Wonderland Trail?" I ask hopefully.

"Yeah, we just started today," one says. They look like I felt after my first climb on the trail—pretty beat.

"Awesome, I'm on day nine! Are you having the best time?" I'm hideously cheerful. Apparently, I needed the reset of a hot shower more than I realized.

"We are having a great time. You look pretty clean for day nine." They both laugh.

"Oh, I had a shower," I explain.

"Are there showers?" Her eyes brighten at the prospect.

"Well, not really. I ran into a friend, and she let me shower in employee housing," I confess.

"Ahh, you have the hookup," she says with a wink.

"Can we be friends today? Where are you ladies headed tomorrow?"

"Yeah, we can definitely be friends today—I'm Charlotte and this is my cousin, Amanda. We are camping at... Dick Creek tomorrow." Charlotte is shorter than me, blonde, and lively with a wide joyous smile which is clearly a permanent fixture. Amanda is taller with dark hair and strong mom energy. Her mid-western accent reminds me instantly of my mom's side of the family.

We walk and talk all the way to Sunrise Campground, and they set up in the site next to mine. I busy myself around my tent for a while with not much to be busy about. Once I've allowed them space to get settled, I take my dinner preparation up to their campsite.

Charlotte explains that she's thru-hiking and Amanda is with her for just the first few days. Charlotte will be joined by her wife when Amanda heads home. This plan must have taken a lot of coordination to put together. Amanda has flown in from Michigan for the occasion and is suffering from the sudden change in altitude. They're in high spirits, nothing cures the difficult hiking blues like crappy trail food and a stranger insisting you are now best friends.

They're so friendly and accommodating that the thought I might be intruding on their cousin bonding time barely crosses my mind. We share stories about our lives and backpacking with comfortable familiarity. I know I will remember these ladies. I don't feel angsty and unsure of myself. I don't wonder if I'm cool enough to be here, I'm just being.

Chapter 10

I REGISTERED FOR A WILDERNESS FIRST RESPONDER (WFR) CLASS in Portland, Oregon to learn the basics of how to handle an emergency while backpacking or rock climbing. I hoped to be better equipped to respond in case of my own injury or illness wandering the world alone. I was also considering becoming a hiking or backpacking guide. This of course, would take place in a fantasy land where I was an impressively strong hiker who didn't nearly collapse at the end of every steep ascent.

During the second week of the WFR training, the class of thirty assembled in the grass of a public city park to be given instruction as to the "scenario" we were walking into. We'd driven up to the scene of a car accident in the middle of nowhere. The vehicle was flipped over and there were people scattered around. We were to locate, assess, and care for each patient until further assistance arrived. We'd been training for this all week.

Minutes later, I sat in a small circle of rescuers huddled around a patient whose white t-shirt was stained with blood. We tried desperately to calm the patient, but he thrashed and yelled out through the park.

"Jacob! Jacob, where are you?" His voice pierced the air and people from other rescue groups glanced over to see what was going on. "Jacob, are you okay? Answer me!"

I scanned around to take inventory of the other clusters of rescuers, each gathered around a passenger of the ill-fated tour group, spread over several hundred yards. This Jacob person could be anywhere.

"Vincent, hold on, hold still. Look at me," I commanded.

I saw how difficult it was for him to stop searching the surroundings and focus on my face with his one good eye. The urgency in every inch of his body spoke of a desperation I could only imagine. Vincent was just another classmate in the WFR course, I'd sat across from him all week. But he had changed, his acting was so convincing that he had worked his own heart rate up to 100 beats per minute.

"Vincent, I'm going to find out where Jacob is, and I'll come back. Please let them help you while I'm gone."

"Please find him, please. I need to know he's okay. It's all that matters," Vincent pleaded.

I thought of the love behind that statement. A man so concerned with his partner's well-being he wouldn't even allow rescuers to splint his badly broken collarbone.

I found Jacob close by, but he looked bad. His rescue team was tightly circled around his prone form. Compared to the fight his partner was putting up, Jacob was downright complacent—his eyelids drooped, and his breathing appeared shallow. His rescuers whispered in urgent tones and I couldn't hear what they were saying as I approached.

"Hey, is your patient's name Jacob?" My words preceded me into the scene.

"Yeah, but we haven't been able to get much more

information from him," one of the rescuers admitted.

"I think we have his husband—over there. Can I give him a status report?" I asked.

"Look, it's not good, but maybe he can help us get some patient history information?" The eager look on the rescuer's face seemed inappropriate. He obviously hadn't noticed the battle being waged between Vincent and my team. I walked back across the field with only a scrap of information for my patient.

"Please let me see him, I need to see him," Vincent begged.

I knelt beside a broken man, his body crumpled and exhausted, like a child worn out from their own crying. I looked pleadingly to the tiny woman restraining him, willing her to let him free.

"No. He'll only be in the way, and plus it could be traumatizing to him." She was stern, undeterred.

The words stung, and a thousand cutting remarks flooded my mind.

It could be traumatizing to see the man he loves die. What about the trauma of being physically restrained twenty feet away and unable to hold the hand of his partner as he dies? What about the trauma of knowing his partner died in the hands of strangers, and he didn't even have the chance to tell him goodbye?

I averted my stinging eyes, fighting to regain my composure. When it became obvious the flood gates had opened despite my best efforts, I stood and walked away from the patient and my fellow rescuers. There was nowhere for me to go. Everywhere I looked rescuers surrounded patients—monitoring vitals and binding broken bones, awaiting news, awaiting transport to definitive care. Less than ten feet away, Jacob lay dying near the base of a tree, four of my classmates gathered around, pantomiming CPR in turns. He was unconscious by this time. The opportunity to say goodbye to his partner had slipped through our blue, rubber-gloved fingers.

If the blood soaking our patient's t-shirt had been real, I would like to think I would have handled the situation differently. If our patient's protests hadn't been interrupted by another rescuer's impatient insistence that we continue through the script, despite the very real human drama playing out in front of us, perhaps I could have convinced a real first responder to do the right thing—the compassionate thing.

I looked up into the lush green canopy above me and let the tears stream down my face. My shoulders shook as I wrapped my arms around myself. I tried to become smaller, to shrink myself into invisibility. The rescuers and patients acted out a scene which must have been alarming to the confused families looking on from the playground.

I saw my father in Vincent's eyes, hopeless with grief, crying out in pain. The loss I had run away from had followed me across the country. In that moment, I knew it would follow me across the world. I had vowed not to end up like my mom, not to cause or suffer the pain of love lost. For it can't possibly be better to have loved and lost—nobody could look my father in the face and say it could.

———

A week later I reclined in a patch of fluffy vivid green grass, each individual blade tickled my elbows as I leaned back. The weight of my body sank into the soft dirt. The sun cast its beams through the canopy above and found my face as I squinted out over the parking lot of the small city park. Cars rarely passed by in this sleepy part of town as I consumed the pages of whichever novel or self-help book I had grabbed off the stack that day. The weather wouldn't hold out for long. The Pacific Northwest isn't known for long, lazy summers, so I reveled in the days of sun that Oregon had bestowed upon me.

I had long imagined Portland would suit me, but upon closer examination, it wasn't so special. There was nothing about this city that made it more desirable than Denver. Swanky coffee shops with pricey organic avocado toasts and chai lattes with macadamia milk lined the streets. Hip young professionals rode fixed gear bicycles from work to the gym, one designer pant leg cuffed to avoid destruction by bike chain. Cute single engineers who were funny and charming commiserated about how they hated their jobs and shared overpriced condos with other job-hating millennials.

I swiped right on those engineers and went on dates for Thai food. I even applied for a Human Resources job I might hate; I considered blending into the fabric of the city. In my dating and business outfits I may have seemed presentable at first glance, but on further inspection that illusion would falter as I had neglected to style my hair or put on makeup.

Cities weren't made for people like me. Or perhaps it was I who was ill-made. I found it difficult during those months to find a place I felt comfortable; often making rounds in the van throughout the day, testing out different parks and neighborhoods. My freedom had become my prison, I was alone in a new way. Far from my friends and my father, I tried to find something uniquely mine. I only found things which belonged to strangers. Places which were somehow owned already, which didn't have any space left for me.

I spent an evening with the engineer and his friends but felt like an impostor.

"Where are you from?" they asked.

"Nowhere really."

"What do you do?" they inquired.

"Everything and nothing."

"Have you seen the latest episode of...?" Their voices became muffled to my ears as I floated off into space.

"I think I'm ready to go," I whispered.

The engineer walked with me under the orange glow of streetlamps to Celeste. She sat benignly on the city street blending into the night. We stood outside the van, kissing and panting. It felt as though my existence was a novelty to him. Something new and different, but impractical. He reminded me countless times he wasn't interested in a relationship, wasn't looking for a commitment.

I allowed him the closeness of a tongue on my neck and a hand up my shirt. His primal desire was exhilarating. To invite him into my home felt strangely inappropriate. He eagerly begged access to my strange life but seemed uninterested in understanding who I was.

Men who found me attractive and unusual were commonplace. They wanted to touch me and taste me. I was nothing more than an amusing departure, an experience to be had. At first it had been convenient to me, to feel the closeness of another body, without having to fear they would get too close.

But these days, a longing was sneaking into my heart. I told myself it was a longing for learning, a longing for greater independence or to figure out who I truly was. But maybe it was a desire to feel at home in someone's presence. My family had moved repeatedly through my childhood leaving me geographically unattached.

Now I searched endlessly for a place that felt like home,

and nowhere felt quite right.

———

A few weeks later I gazed into a pair of green eyes. They were new to me, but familiar, sad. I had been in Portland the better part of a month and had been reading a book at the botanic garden when he asked me to come over. Sitting amidst the plants which didn't belong together, I felt out of place. They were groomed into neat little rows and floral arrangements with tiny placards giving them names chosen by long-ago explorers and naturalists. I was far less ordered, far less precise, far less identified. I had left the strange compilation of rare and exotic flowers, bushes, and trees to go back into the city.

In Tom's small bedroom, we laid together on a mattress on the floor. Our loneliness brought us together, and the peace of the afternoon settled in around us. He asked why I was in Portland. I tried to explain but came up short. I talked myself in circles about independence and looking for a place to call home. He wanted to know why I felt so lost in the world.

"I think I don't know who I am anymore. Since my mom died, I don't have her to compare myself to. I heard often as a girl, how like her I was. There are these photos of both of us around two years old, we look exactly the same. She's in black and white, with perfect little curls. I've got one of those plastic rings from a stacking toy around my ankle. I wanted to be just like her when I grew up. Then I grew up. At some point I started to see all the ways I didn't want to be like her. Then she just went and died. I didn't have time to reconcile who she was as a person. Or to figure out who I was without her. She's just gone." The words tumbled out of me. It was a relief to have them out of my head.

Embarrassment burned my cheeks as I realized that Tom

was looking down while I spoke. I was oversharing. He didn't want to get into a serious conversation about mortality and identity with me. We didn't know each other like that.

When he raised his eyes to meet mine, they were wet.

"My mom is really sick right now," he said. "She probably isn't going to make it. I've been too afraid to go visit her. To see her like that. It's just too hard to think about losing her."

My stomach tightened with regret. "Oh. I'm so sorry."

I put my arms around him again. Suddenly, we knew each other.

Day 10: August 11, 2018
Sunrise Camp → Mystic Camp

I HIT THE TRAIL EARLY WITH CHARLOTTE AND AMANDA UNDER A steely gray sky, a light mist hanging in the air. I grumble at the shift in the weather before acknowledging to myself that, after so many sunny days, I should endure with grace. As we establish a slow and steady pace, I feel refreshed and energized, my legs powering beneath me without complaint.

We rotate order throughout the morning, at times close enough to hold a three-way conversation, at others drifting far enough apart to feel a sense of solitude. Our brightly colored rain jackets act as beacons through the dense fog, reassuring us that we haven't lost each other along the trail.

At White River the water is deep and roiling and a shiny, newly placed log bridge stands above it.

"This is the river people drowned in last week, right?" I ask, knowing full well from the big ominous circle on my map, this is that river.

"I hadn't heard." Charlotte raises her eyebrows, and we all exchange nervous looks.

"Apparently a couple of people died crossing this river,"

I explain, "but it looks like this is the new bridge, with handrails." I gesture at the wooden handrails sticking out at a strange angle from the log. The river surges beneath and, for the first time today, I count us lucky for the clouds and cool weather. They provide respite from the record temperatures which have caused dangerous glacial melt in the previous weeks.

As Amanda prepares to cross, she unclips the chest strap on her backpack and transfers her trekking poles to her right wrist. Grasping the handrail firmly with her left hand, she proceeds slowly across. Charlotte and I wait on the ground until she safely reaches the other side. Charlotte follows next, and I mimic their preparations.

If I were hiking alone, I wouldn't have thought to unclip my pack. I'm embarrassed of my ignorance. If I fall in the water, my chances of swimming to safety will be greatly improved if I can escape the straps. My peers model good practices that I should already know.

With slow, cautious steps I cross the log bridge. Charlotte and Amanda wait for me to reach them so we can share enthusiastic high fives before continuing up the trail. After some debate we decide to stop and have a snack, though it's tempting to push on without a break since the fog has turned to a steady drizzle. Longer miles with fewer breaks would mean more time sitting around camp or lying in a sleeping bag. All of which is perfectly lovely if campfires or cuddle buddies are available, but I have neither. My time is better spent eating a granola bar and laughing with friends. This afternoon, they will leave me at Mystic Lake and continue to Dick Creek.

I'm reminded of a much wetter day on the Appalachian Trail. It was the first week of April, and my jacket was doing a poor job of keeping me dry in the driving rain. I'd been hiking for several hours when I came to an unmarked road crossing. Earlier in the day, hikers had been discussing an alternate route to avoid the next summit. I was considering it—mostly because of the weather, but also because I was exhausted and doubting myself and felt like a break would do me some good.

However, I wasn't about to wander up some unnamed logging road alone without one hundred percent certainty this was, in fact, the road I was looking for. I stood at the intersection paralyzed by doubt. There was nobody else around and tears welled in my eyes. At my own indecision, at my weakness, and at the idea that on a 2,000-mile trail, I was considering skipping a one-mile section because it was raining. I plopped down on a tree stump and dug a cookie out of my pack. I flipped to the page of my AT guide and studied the elevation profile, trying to psych myself up for the next summit.

Flipping the book closed on my lap, I finished my cookie and shut my eyes. With a few deep breaths, I reminded myself that not only had I chosen to be there, I was lucky to have the opportunity. When I opened my eyes, a couple of hikers and a dog walked toward me on the trail. I rearranged my face into forced pleasantness. It was the loud and abrasive woman from the bar in Franklin and I didn't want to join her and her partner up the next section of trail. After they passed, I figured I could make my slow ascent and not cross paths with them again until after the summit.

As they approached the woman called out, "Sitting there crying about it won't make it any easier."

The comment was so shockingly abrasive that I didn't respond. I waited as they continued along the trail, mentally screaming curses at her back and hoping more fervently than ever to spend the rest of the day alone.

―――――

"Do you want one? I have way too many snacks." I'm brought back to reality by Charlotte holding out her bag of treats.

"Oh, no thanks, I'll be back to civilization in two days. You're only just getting started!"

We gather our things and sling our packs back on, the rain still falling lightly around us.

We walk in silence for some time. With my hood around my face, the world is a little smaller. My field of view is boxed in by a thick line of turquoise, so I concentrate on the trail in front of me.

"Can I ask you something?" Charlotte breaks the silence.

"Yeah, of course," I say.

"Do you ever worry about what people think? Like what people think about what you do? Like your dad, people you know..." Her voice trails off.

Do I ever!

"My dad told me a long time ago that he didn't understand what I was trying to accomplish, but he wanted me to be happy. And not to ask him for money." We laugh, but my heart sinks. "I've tried to explain to him that I don't want to look back on my life and wonder why I didn't go after my dreams. He doesn't really get it."

"But your mom would be proud of you," Charlotte offers charitably.

I agree without conviction, "yeah."

My mom had different dreams for me, different priorities. She used to say, "it's not what you say, but how you say it." Perhaps she wouldn't be disappointed that what I'm doing is so different than what she wanted for me. She would be disappointed at how I'm doing it. She wouldn't understand why I insist on wandering the world alone. I decided a long time ago that I would rather suffer the pain of loneliness than the pain of love. I don't think she would have understood that. It's cowardly really.

She built a beautiful world around herself. She chose to leave behind the family she was born into and find one of her own. She found love and comfort in my father and his family and what they created. She used to say, "I could be happy anywhere, as long as I'm with your dad." She wasn't interested in seeing the world or pushing boundaries. She had what she needed.

I never had to hike these hundred miles—it hasn't proved a thing. I am still the woman I was eleven days ago. I am no less my mother's daughter than I was before I began. To walk this path alone has only proven my own stubbornness, my need to cling to this mistake because it's been so long in the making. When I get back in my van and look into the mirror, my mother's eyes will still look back at me. When I comb my hair and scowl at my jiggly thighs, she will still be there. And when I get back to Denver, to the family I have found, she will be there too.

"Hey, thanks for letting me hang with you ladies. This has been truly lovely," I say from behind.

Charlotte turns around with a look of surprise on her face. Sometimes the simplest truths are difficult to put into words, so we avoid doing so. Telling someone you so recently met that you are enjoying spending time with them can come across as weird or desperate, but I don't know if I will ever see these women again. Another family I will leave behind.

At Mystic Lake, the sun breaks the clouds for the first time all day. The light peers through the trees, and I catch a warm beam on my face as we say goodbye. We stand together on the sandy lake side, admiring the blue-green water reflecting the trees and mountains back with perfect detail. The heavy gray clouds which have been looming all day are now drifting out of sight, and fluffy white ones are taking their place.

This is the last lake I will see on my hike. At the end of a cold, rainy day, I'm not overwhelmed by the desire to plunge into this lake, but I stand knee deep in the cool water.

"Come on, put your feet in!" I call.

"No, we still have miles to go. I don't want to take my shoes off." Amanda expresses a feeling that's all too familiar to me.

As they walk on, I am sad for all the lakes I never put my feet in, sad for all the side trails I never hiked, the waterfalls I never stood beneath. The journey of becoming a person willing to wander from the direct path in order to take joy in the non-productive is slow and steady. It may not get me any closer to the "goal" or the "end", but to stand in this lake, goosebumps raised on my arms and legs, is to more deeply experience the ecstasy which comes with a short respite from a gloomy day.

———

I find a log next to the lake and settle in with my new book, trying to soak up as much sun as possible before nightfall. The memoir opens with some discussion of the dynamics of being a female climbing ranger in Mt. Rainier National Park, and I find the author and her stories instantly relatable. She writes about toughing it out in uncomfortable situations, never complaining, never showing weakness because she knows she must work twice as hard to prove her worth as a woman. She also recounts being interviewed about her job but being asked questions focused on her gender rather than her profession.

While I'm reading, a ranger stops through and asks to see my permit. I show him the paper, which I happen to be using as a bookmark. We exchange pleasantries and he continues on his way. It occurs to me now that while the rangers I interacted with in the ranger stations were all women, both of those I have seen out on the trail have been men. The author of the book complains that she and her female colleagues rarely got assigned to rescue missions and were often left staffing the front desk at the climbing center. Perhaps it's "too dangerous" for women to be out on the mountain, confronting rule breakers and braving the elements.

My mind then shifts to Judah. I wonder if he has run into any more rangers since we parted ways. Where is he now? Has he finished his hike? Even in the connected world in which we live, the answer to these questions will forever remain a mystery to me.

Another cluster of gray clouds move in and obscure the sun. The temperature drops, and I hug my fleece jacket tightly around my waist. It's still early in the afternoon when I head back to my tent for shelter. Curled up in my down sleeping bag, I listen to the sprinkles falling on the nylon rain fly over my head. The pattering of rain is soothing and rhythmic as I alternate between reading and dozing throughout the afternoon. I hungrily consume the smell of wet earth that permeates the walls of my tent.

These are the moments I both cherish and bemoan being alone. To be lazy and cozy alone and without judgment is comfortable and pure. But to be lazy and cozy together would be warm and comforting. I play in my mind how different it would be to share this moment with somebody, lying together reading books and staying dry on a rainy day.

Cooking oatmeal for two and snuggling up with steaming cups of tea. A shared sense of adventure makes light of a dark day, and a shared tent makes warmth of a cold night.

I read of a young woman feeling beaten down in a dream job which didn't live up to her expectations. I wonder if my dream togetherness would perhaps not live up to my expectations either. Perhaps I would long for the days when I backpacked solo, answering to no desires but my own. In all likelihood, I'm one of those cranky people who is never satisfied with what they have and takes for granted all they have been afforded in life.

The sky is darkening when I turn the last page of the book and realize that I've read the entire thing cover to cover in one day. The stories are relatable and sometimes funny, but I had been hoping for something more.

The author makes reference to the difficulties of being a woman in a man's world but at the end of the story, I'm left wanting. Wanting her to stand up to the oppressor who won't provide proper shoes for the task at hand, proper pay for the dangerous and exhausting work, and fair assignment of duties. I want her to tell me that being a strong independent woman is worth the struggle, that she kicked ass and came out on top. But alas, the happy ending is just that she left the shitty dream job, and what kind of consolation prize is that?

I sleep fitfully, waking a dozen times during the night with cramping legs and sore hips. The sound of rain never ceases, and my body grows restless as the hours suspended in repose crawl by.

Chapter 11

I WANDERED THE CITY ON THE FOURTH OF JULY, TRYING TO FIND A PLACE for my body. The air hung damp and heavy and my usually serene park hangouts were crowded with barbecues and sparklers. Children ran and screamed while red, white and blue clad adults stood around drinking beers. I'm not much for celebrating holidays, but the day seemed particularly obtuse because I couldn't even ignore the holiday in peace. I had nowhere to go.

When the sun finally set, I drove to a favorite parking spot in the suburbs. Across from a small local park and behind a row of condominiums, the street lined with cars felt humble and nondescript. I had slept uninterrupted at that location a half dozen nights in the past month. With my reflective window shades in place, I climbed into the back of the van. The cracking and booming of exploding fireworks rang in my ears. I thought about my father, probably cursing the neighbors from his couch, begrudging them the right to celebrate and enjoy themselves like he used to. Having become accustomed to the sounds of the road and the heat of the summer, I fell asleep atop my thick fleece blanket.

Suddenly, my eyes snapped open. My heart raced, and the hairs stood at attention on every inch of my body. My brain sluggishly struggled to discern what had woken me.

Thump thump thump thump.

Something tapped the outside of the van, less than three feet from where I lay stock still. I tried to control my breathing, but the adrenaline coursed through my body with an intensity which could hardly be contained by my skin.

Thump thump thump thump.

The tapping came in perfect rhythm as though someone was idly knocking as they walked by, perhaps humming a tune under their breath.

What the fuck? Are they checking to see if someone is inside? Are they going to break in? Are they thieves or murderers? Is this how I die?

I squinted but couldn't make out a shadow outside the window. I couldn't peer around the curtain for fear that whoever was outside might notice the movement.

Maybe my dad was right, maybe I should be carrying a gun.

Thump thump thump thump.

I swallowed hard, but the lump in my throat was the proverbial immovable object and the swallowing of my fear scarcely registered as a force at all.

Should I dial 911? Is someone fucking with me? Could I get out of bed and drive away before they broke in?

The thumping continued in regular intervals and its precision made it all the more menacing. Each pause between rounds felt like the void of eternal possibility. I concentrated on the noise, frantically racking my brain for some logical explanation, when I recognized the unmistakable stuttering ratcheting hiss of a sprinkler head.

Thump thump thump thump.

The sound of the sprinkler and the water hitting the side of the van were a soothing duet. They sang a song of reassurance, of safety, of confidence. They hushed the voice in my head that knows there is danger everywhere I go, simply because I am a woman. A woman alone.

To live my life on high alert is a choice I made, traveling unchaperoned. I assess my surroundings constantly, take inventory of the people around me, make note of their physical descriptions, where their hands are, how long it would take them to reach me and how quickly I could get somewhere safe. I watch them when they think I'm not paying attention and I think about whether I have the guts to gouge their eyes out with a key or my thumbs, like I learned in self-defense.

There are things I avoid because they are too high risk, like getting gas after dark in an unknown town and listening to music while I run. I refuse to sacrifice the joy of life and expansion to the burden of being safe in a dangerous world. I've heard stories of women being raped and murdered in their home, so does making a vehicle my home make the risk any higher? I have been assaulted twice in a city I called home, so it's difficult to believe that wandering the world puts me at any greater danger.

———

Laura called as the heat of the summer was beginning to melt my brain. I felt stagnant and suffocated, the humidity and temperatures weighing me down day and night. I was like a drifter circling the city, but I struggled to find a reason to leave. Without a next destination, how does one press on?

"Do you want to drive up and meet me at Mt. Rainier?" Laura asked. "I'm going to Seattle for a few days and I thought I would check it out on the way."

"Yes, I'll be there." I didn't hesitate.

Laura and I met in Sunrise and hiked a short trail to a lookout tower. We stopped several times along the way to stare at Mt. Rainier. Laura proclaimed with absolute authority, "That's a good-looking mountain." I seconded her assessment.

"Would you ever want to climb it?" She waggled her eyebrows.

"I've never been interested in mountaineering," I say, "but now that I'm looking at it, I understand why people climb big mountains."

Mt. Rainier posed proudly before us, its snowy peak rising impressively from the rolling hills on which we stood. It was magnificent and unassuming all at once. Mt. Rainier didn't care what I thought of it, and it thought nothing of me. I felt so connected and full, as if this mountain and all it touched were somehow a part of me—but also small and insignificant, for I would never learn all its secrets or truly understand its life.

After a long while, we turned in silence and started back toward the car. We passed a small wooden sign at a trail crossing: *Wonderland Trail*. I had heard of it before, as a short thru-hike, but didn't know any of the details.

"Maybe I should come hike the Wonderland Trail," I proposed.

"Yes, you definitely should!" she agreed.

Since the day we met, Laura's faith in me had been unwavering. Her belief in my ability to hike Mt Whitney may have been blind or naïve. Her encouragement meant more now. I knew that she knew me well and wouldn't steer me wrong. I also knew that she believed I could do anything, and that helped me believe it too.

After a couple days in Seattle, the Wonderland Trail still felt like the next thing for me. To run away into the woods, to see Wonderland for myself. I don't know what I hoped to find out there. Perhaps if I could find my own piece of Wonderland and bring it back with me, I could finally find a place to settle. Or a person to call home.

Day 11: August 12, 2018
Mystic Camp → Carbon River

IT'S EASY TO GET AN EARLY START WHEN THE SUN IS OUT, AND THE RAIN has finally stopped. Sometime late last night, I decided that today would be my last day of hiking. The miles from Mystic Camp to Mowich Lake should be easily passed in one day. I can't quite say if it was the rain which caused me to long for the hard walls of my van, or if I'm just ready to charge my phone and tell my friends how much I've missed them.

An unfamiliar sound breaches the barriers of my rambling thoughts. I've been tromping through the forest for the better part of the morning. The sightline in all directions is obstructed by trees which appear to be thinning up ahead. As I proceed, the mysterious sounds grow more distinct: cracking like thunder—not louder but definitely closer. When I focus on the noise, it's almost non-stop—sharp cracks broken up by a constant creaking and crunching. A humming vibration in the air shakes my bones.

I round the next corner and am greeted with an unmatched view. The Carbon River is flowing madly in front of me. In many ways, it's not unlike Mt Rainier's other glacial rivers—surging, milky brown water flows aggressively over boulders and shows off its formidable power as the sun melts the glacier feeding it. The unmistakable difference is the proximity to the glacier, which looms only a hundred or so feet from the trail. This glacial ice connects to the entire system that composes the summit of the mountain.

The snout of Carbon Glacier is close to 11,000 vertical feet and six miles from the summit of Mt Rainier. On the Mt Rainier Wilderness Trip Planner Map, the system of glaciers resembles a many-legged octopus centered atop the mountain with its tentacles stretching out in every direction. Of the twenty-five named glaciers, Carbon reaches the furthest and the lowest. It's long and skinny with an elegantly curving two-pronged tongue at its terminus like the tip of a cartoon flame.

I look up to the summit of Mt Rainier standing proudly above. This river has wandered far and away from its source but is still inextricably connected. Carbon Glacier has stretched itself thin, trying to escape its roots entirely. Non-attachment to the source is impossible. Without connection, the river would simply dry up and cease to exist. But what would become of Carbon River if Mt Rainier had been the one to leave?

I stand at the edge, the point at which the furthest familial relation fractures and violently calves away into a roiling gush of water. Headed off toward the Pacific Ocean by way of the Puyallup River and then Puget Sound. These last few years, I've broken away, searching for a place to call home and a sense of self that wasn't defined by my relationship to my mother. I have resisted the truth since the day my mother left this world. She isn't coming back. Our physical connection is irrevocably severed. I am no longer defined by the way she sees me. I can no longer disappoint her, make her proud, or break her heart. There are more options in this life than fulfilling her expectations or defying them.

I've felt the lonely pull of a stranger's arms and the defiant desire to walk away from people who remind me of the family I once belonged to. This has been my melting point. I was ice, but now I'm water. The breaking away has been savage, painful, loud and traumatic. I was part of something solid and corporeal, but it couldn't stay that way forever. Nobody forewarned that my dissolution into the ocean of the world was an inevitability. But the journey from glacier to ocean is not one from something to nothing.

Epilogue

WHEN I SET FOOT ON THE WONDERLAND TRAIL, I ASKED A QUESTION.
Why am I alone?
But it was the wrong question. I knew why I was alone.
I had gone out of my way to be alone. Some people I had
pushed away, some I had left. Some had left me. But I had
always worked toward my own loneliness, had devised its
existence.

The real question was something more complicated.

*If independence is such a noble pursuit, then why am I so
unhappy?*

Because I had proclaimed "independent" as part of my
identity. I had been made to believe that independence is a
strength. Self-reliance is an admirable quality. I should find
joy within. And all that other inspirational tripe. And I had
held tightly to it, allowing it to stand in the way of all other
pursuits.

I spent eleven days walking around Mt Rainier. Admiring
her strength, her strange independence. The way she rises
from almost nothing. She stands proudly and looks down
on all around her. But she is also deeply interconnected. It is

one thing to face the mountain and see her solitary glory, and another to turn around and see all that holds her up.

As it turns out, independence is not an identity. Identity is built on our relationships to others. To identify as independent, I am only defining my relationship to others as separate. It means nothing without a point of reference.

Identity isn't found in aloneness, but in self-knowledge. When I quit drinking, I uncovered the woman who had been hiding beneath the fog of alcohol and the disconnection it caused. When I hiked the Appalachian Trail, my identity blossomed because for the first time, I was about something. I called myself a backpacker and became part of a community. When I started running, identity grew within me as I pushed myself further than I ever had to find my limit. It took a few years before I claimed the title "runner" and joined another community.

―――――

It wasn't until I returned to Denver that this all started to become clear. I reconnected to the world I had left behind. I saw familiar faces for the first time in months. I watched as the maple tree outside my old window turned from green to red.

I called Lindy.

The loss of her mom only eight months before had been hanging over us since my return. She was still wading through her grief, trying her best to keep moving forward. I was unsure of how to broach the subject, because of the guilt I felt for not being there sooner. Too much time had passed, I should have been there for her. I was the one who knew what it was to lose my mother.

Over the next few weeks, we spoke endlessly of our mothers. In this, we found new identity in our relationship with each other. We told stories of our childhoods and of our mothers' love. We confessed our regrets and our resentments. Saying them aloud for the first time, and in some cases admitting them to ourselves for the first time.

Slowly, our identities became entwined. I knew myself better for knowing Lindy, and for revealing myself to her. She became the person in this world who knows me best. She knows my history, my purpose, my heart. She is the person I call when I don't know what to do. She is the person I call when I'm not sure who I am.

We are our mothers' daughters.

But we see the artist, writer, poet, runner, climber, yogi, clown, backpacker, woman, mother, sister, child, best friend in each other.

Dad,

I know it wasn't easy for you to read this book. And you were not the first person along this journey to ask if I was sure I wanted to expose myself to the world in this way. But without this book, I would likely have never found the courage to speak openly to you about the path my life has taken, and now I have. For that, I have no regrets.

I can imagine how painful it must be to know that all your efforts couldn't protect me from the world or from myself. I'm sure many parents have felt that pain. It's one of the reasons that I don't know if I could be a parent. But I hope that seeing me more fully might give you the context to understand how I became the person I am today, and why I had to do the things I did.

I am not the woman you and mom meant for me to be. I know that. But I have finally found my way to happy and whole. It may have taken unconventional methods to get here. But I did it. And not without falling back on the values you instilled in me as a child. It wasn't academic excellence that helped me find my way, but a love of growth and learning. And it wasn't financial responsibility that showed me what I was made of, but an unflagging work ethic and focus on a goal.

When I decided it was time to move forward from my mess, I knew that I could because you had told me I could do anything I set my mind to. And even through every decision I've made that you didn't agree with or understand, you've always come back to that. When I told you that I was writing this book, you honestly believed that I would. And that it would be a success. And not just in the eye-rolling, placating way that most parents would encourage their child to write a book. You really meant it.

There were times during this process that your belief was the only thing that kept me moving forward. I didn't want to let you down. I didn't know that you had always been interested in writing a book. Sometimes I'm reminded that we are more alike than I give us credit for.

I'm sorry this book was hard for you to read. It wasn't easy to write. But you helped.

Acknowledgments

A special thanks to Lindy—my best friend, my mahm, my editor, and my muse. Without you, this book would have far too many commas and not a single dash. Your friendship has always been thoughtful and intentional, when we have lived together and apart. I simply would not be the woman I am today if we had never met.

Thank you to Laura, for telling me about Mt Whitney. For the days spent cooking in Huff and knitting at the Ahwahnee. For asking me to stay in Denver. For showing me that homeownership is possible. For inviting me to Mt Rainier. And for always believing in my ability to do literally any crazy thing I tell you I'm going to do.

To my partner, Ryan, who has only ever known me as an author and has believed in this project since the day we met. Your faith in my abilities has filled in when my own has faltered. For the months I laid in your bed reading stacks of memoirs and adventure stories, during which you repeatedly marveled at how "productive" I was being, thank you.

Thank you to Melanie, for the fake deadlines when I needed to be held accountable. To Greg and Eddie for reading messy, early iterations of disjointed stories directly from my brain spout. To Adam for working so thoroughly through the final version, and reminding me that not everybody thinks I'm as funny as I think I am. To Lois and Doug for rescuing a stranded and very smelly hiker from her broken down (again) van.

To all the hikers and bystanders that have made their way into the story of my life. Your real names may not appear in print, but your impact is indelible.

To both of my amazing editors, Tracy Gold and Nikki Rae Jensen, for helping to make this story the best that it could be. To my photographer and friend, Jay Dallas, for making me look good and for letting me pay you way too late. To my graphic designer, Chris Greco (not gecko), for his excellent artistic vision and execution. Thank you.

I've heard that this part is the hardest to write. There are so many people who've leant an ear, an eye, and a pen to this work, and I should have been making a list as I went along. To everyone who offered an encouraging word, with or without reading any of the drafts along the way, your heart is in this book. Thank you so much.

A note to the reader:

This is a story about my life. The people, events, and places within are portrayed to the best of my memory. While all the stories are true, most names and many identifying details have been changed to protect the privacy of people involved. Dialogue is not meant to represent a word-for-word transcript of conversations, as I do not carry a tape recorder on my person. Rather, I have retold them in a way that evokes the feeling and meaning of what was said, to my recollection. Small liberties may have been taken with the chronology of events, to suit the flow of the story.